educate and inspire others to invest in their own financial education. His devotion to his family, his friends, and his mission to change the way we think about money is unparalleled. His latest work, The Lost Science of Compound Interest, *is the first book I read three times, back to back to back. I couldn't put it down. It is truly a breath of fresh air. Don't just read it once as the financial knowledge is like nothing ever presented before. The words will become the foundation for your future self!*

—Eric Palmer, CMO, Brokers Alliance, Fountain Hills, AZ

"Having worked in the financial services industry for nearly a decade, I thought I had the system pretty well figured out. I worked for the financial giant, Vanguard, and believed in the low-cost index funds as the "best" option for myself and my clients. I had my next 30 years planned out. I contributed heavily to my 401k and got the generous company match. I was fully convinced the 4% Rule for income was the best retirement outcome I could expect. Then I heard about Curtis Ray and MPI™. I had never heard the things that Curtis shared with me. It even sounded a little crazy. How was it possible to increase

your growth rate as you got older, not decrease it, as I had come to accept as the standard? As Curtis began to explain the concept of Secure Compound Interest, it all began to make sense. We, as the financial advising community, had been looking at compounding from the wrong direction the whole time. Curtis's MPI™ system brought together many of the things that I believed in while introducing concepts I didn't know could synergize the way he showed me. It turned my world upside down. After learning the things I learned, I couldn't continue to participate in the traditional methods I had previously embraced. I went all-in on MPI™, both for my career and my own retirement strategy. Nothing else compares."

—Chris Hale, Financial Advisor, COO SunCor Financial, Mesa, AZ

"I've been in the financial services industry for over two decades and have seen almost everything in my career. I was one of the biggest proponents to Infinite Banking Concept/ Bank on Yourself and felt that was the best system for my clients. MPI™ changed all of that and is like nothing I've ever come across. What does it mean when someone says the words, Game Changer? It's an expression used when something significant changes the course of a game. It's also used in business when an idea or an invention changes how we do things forever. Using leverage isn't necessarily new to the business world, but the way in which it is implemented using the MPI™ program talked about in this book does make it a Game Changer. The ease in which you can implement an all-in -one, automated process, to leverage a life insurance policy at the policy level is innovative and exciting. Now, everyone who wants to create wealth can—it's that simple—it's a Game Changer for anyone wanting to save and compound safely and build wealth for their future, all with significant tax-advantages."

—**Dan Thompson, Financial Educator, CEO of Wise Money Tools, Eagle, ID**

"After a decade of self-employment, I had almost given up on reaching the level of financial security I desired. I watched brilliant business owners breaking their backs and their bank accounts to match the mindset of Tony Robbins, the attitude of Gary Vaynerchuk, the selling skills of Sara Blakely, the work ethic of Grant Cardone, and the marketing expertise of Russell Brunson, only to come up short. The takeaway devastated me: we can't all be industry giants.

"Then I met Curtis Ray, and he taught me the Laws of Wealth and why I keep under-performing. It changed every aspect of my life. Because of his innovative financial strategies and his mission to save the world, the future of my family is more secure than I ever could have imagined. Anyone willing to learn and apply the principles Curtis shares in this book will experience the peace and excitement that I have found through MPI™."

—*Zach Garner, Investor, Podcast Host Reaching World, Meridian, ID*

The

LOST SCIENCE

of

COMPOUND INTEREST

Copyright © 2020 by Curtis Ray.

All rights reserved. No part of this publication may be reproduced, distributed, or transmitted in any form or by any means, including photocopying, recording, or other electronic or mechanical methods, without the prior written permission of the author, except in the case of brief quotations embodied in critical reviews and certain other noncommercial uses permitted by copyright law.

Second Edition

ISBN: 978-1-937449-07-0

Ordering Information: Special discounts are available for quantity purchases of this book by corporations, associations, and others. For orders by U.S. trade bookstores and wholesalers, please contact Curtis Ray at www.CurtisRay.com

Table of Contents

CHAPTER 1   The Science of Compound Interest 1

CHAPTER 2   Everyone Ends Up Poor™ 11

CHAPTER 3   Yin and Yang 31

CHAPTER 4   The Wealth Equation: The Exponential Growth Curve ... 41

CHAPTER 5   The Five Paths of Conventional Financial "Freedom" 55

CHAPTER 6   The Evolution of Cash Value Life Insurance 69

CHAPTER 7   Leverage: OPM Made Secure 85

CHAPTER 8   The Pure Compounder 109

CHAPTER 9   MPI™: Good to Great 119

CHAPTER 10   MPI™ to the Test 143

CHAPTER 11   Early Adopters 177

CHAPTER 12   Everyone Ends Up Rich 185

ADDITIONAL TESTIMONIALS 191

AFTERWORD 195

YOUR CUSTOMIZED FINANCIAL PLAN 197

Acknowledgments

My wife, Erin, deserves top gratitude in support of me writing between podcasts, seminars, and keynotes, as well as being a husband, father, and coach. She has sacrificed so much time with me so I could write this book over the last 6 months. Having heard my story at least 10,000 times, she still listens with intrigue and enthusiasm about my life's mission to provide the world with the lost financial knowledge of Pure Compound Interest.

Additional thanks to Chris Hale, my Chief Operating Officer, who joined the SunCor Mission after eight years working at Vanguard, one of the largest financial services companies in the world. He was among the first to leave an established career and become a follower of my theory and philosophy of the ABC of Wealth.

Throughout the country, countless others deserve recognition for their support and belief in my mission; they have become true believers that Compound Interest is not only an energy with immeasurable influence but is also available to anyone who wants it. I appreciate everyone who has taken the time to listen to my passion regarding financial abundance, as well as those who are reading this book to begin their journey to financial freedom.

About the Author

Curtis Ray is the founder, owner, and CEO of SunCor Financial. In 2014, Curtis was introduced to the world of financial planning and insurance. Through years of research, Curtis observed that the traditional investment strategies of the 401(k), IRA, Real Estate, and Life Insurance were not living up to the promises and expectations people were hoping for in retirement. By bringing awareness to the Five Rules of Wealth and their influence on Compound Interest, Curtis is helping hardworking people, from all walks of life, maximize retirement income through discipline, Secure Leverage, and achieve Exponential Growth by becoming a Pure Compounder. He designed and developed the patent pending MPI™ Strategy (Maximum Premium Indexing) to accomplish all Five Rules of Wealth simultaneously, solving the riddle of investing and increasing retirement income by up to 400%.

Throughout his life, Curtis has been a serial entrepreneur, inventor, and Amazon Best-Selling author of the book *Everyone Ends Up Poor!*™. With a passion to take on issues that some accept as status quo, Curtis solves financial inefficiencies by using entirely new approaches.

Prior to founding SunCor Financial, Curtis served a 2-year mission for the Church of Jesus Christ of Latter-day Saints in Santiago, Chile. Upon finishing his mission, Curtis attended Arizona State University and competed on their wrestling team. While still in college, he started his first business in the granite countertop industry, growing the business to more than 60 kitchens per week by 2012. This inspired him to launch his second business for which he designed and developed the patented revolutionary natural stone system called ForzaStone®.

Curtis lives in Gilbert, Arizona, and is married to Erin Ray; they have five beautiful children (Cayden, Caliann, Brody, Lexi, and Kenzie). He enjoys spending time with his family and playing sports, especially football, basketball, and wrestling. Curtis is also an avid world traveler who enjoys experiencing other cultures and history while seeing all that the world has to offer.

Preface

Always Be Compounding! Those three simple words can transform your life into anything you want it to be. This energy force is so powerful that it can fix any problem you might encounter in your life right now. Albert Einstein is credited with saying, "Compound Interest is the most powerful force in the Universe and the 8th Wonder of the World!" Not only is there a defined roadmap for achieving this phenomenon; it's quite simple.

This book will challenge everything you've ever considered (or may have been told) regarding money. Everyone has goals and dreams. Few ever accomplish them because they have been given the wrong blueprint. It has been wrong for a very long time, and generations have bought into it, leading most people to frustration and confusion in their retirement years.

However, the correct roadmap is available to all. It's called slow, steady, and secure—the foundation of Compound Interest.

Foreword

On Thursday, March 21st, 2019, I tuned in to the Feed Me Fuel Me podcast, as I did every Thursday, and heard Curtis Ray for the very first time. As the host opened with the title of Curtis' first book: *Everyone Ends Up Poor! Why Financial Planning is All Backwards and How to Fix It*, they had my full attention. Because I had dedicated nearly twenty years to the financial services industry, much of it advancing the cause of financial empowerment through Financial Planning, Curtis was singing my song. His mission and purpose to serve others, working together to solve the issue of financial independence through a call toward discipline and accountability, was music to my ears.

Following the podcast, I had many more questions; as a CERTIFIED FINANCIAL PLANNER™ professional, the details intensely interested me. I was eager to hear how Curtis had solved so many issues that have dogged Financial Planners when designing a retirement plan. Two things happened within seconds: I texted my friend, Mycal Anders (the host of the podcast), asking for an introduction to Curtis and simultaneously reached out to Curtis on LinkedIn. Curtis replied first, negating the need for an introduction. I was shocked by how quickly Curtis responded, but I later came to appreciate how open he is to questions, comments, dialogue, and conversation.

We spent the spring and summer working together professionally while also becoming friends. Curtis is a kindred spirit in our shared belief that people who work hard, save hard, and have the level of commitment to make solid long-term decisions ought to benefit from their own hard-earned money. That said, I had a clear idea of what a "successful plan" looked like, how most people should prioritize spending in a way that serves them best, and how to optimize success. From a planning perspective, I had consensus-creep in my brain. In fact, in the early months I contacted Curtis multiple times with what I believed was an oversight, a fancy way to say I thought I had a "gotcha" question for him. Curtis being Curtis answered in a non-defensive, confident way having done endless research before launching. Curtis spent hours answering my questions as I moved through the six stages of grief: denial that my education was in question, guilt that I hadn't done what's best for my own spouse, anger that I'd missed what Curtis had seen, reflection on what he was teaching me, strategizing as we worked through my new plan (my very own MPI™), and finally acceptance that what he had built was sound.

Throughout my career working directly with clients, leading branches, and as an executive leader, much focus was routinely placed on serving the wealthy. Curtis was quick to shine a spotlight on the elephant in the room: the wealthy were among the few who could enjoy retirement on their own terms without having to compromise in order to avoid the pervasive fear of running out of money in retirement. Said a different way, only the wealthy could have a dream-retirement using the 4% Rule. And to give credit where it is due, many advisors are doing noble work providing access to professional advice for people that are not considered "high net-worth." Unfortunately, their plan is always the same: a calculation to force decisions that trade away the future you want for the one you can afford.

Here is my suggestion, reader. Before you allow yourself an objection, read through this book at least one time. Then test the math, test the premise, do your research, and ask your questions. There is little doubt that you will find what I found: the math doesn't lie, and Curtis will answer any questions you have. Of course, no one thing is for everyone. My wish for you is that if you learn ONE thing from this book, it is a commitment to think (and act) exponentially!

Wishing you success, financial freedom, and the empowerment to achieve the life you want for yourself and the people you care about.

Ken Kilday, RCC™, CFP®
Executive Business Coach

The
LOST SCIENCE
of
COMPOUND INTEREST

CHAPTER 1

The Science of Compound Interest

Compound Interest! The purest form of money. Beautiful mathematical art that unlocks unlimited wealth potential for anyone who desires it! An energy force so powerful and influential that anyone, regardless of their past, can benefit from it. If you make money, you can build wealth.

Albert Einstein is credited for saying Compound Interest is "The 8th wonder of the world; he who understands it, earns it!" But is it really that powerful? Many have written and talked about it, but why do so few ever achieve its true potential? Because earning it requires that you "understand it." Given what we've all been taught to believe about money by mainstream financial advice, it's fair to say we have lost this knowledge.

My name is Curtis Ray from Gilbert, Arizona. A husband, father, entrepreneur, best-selling author, and money scientist. For 15 years I've worked and invested in business, real estate, stocks, insurance, and various other ventures, all the while researching the optimization of money through the science of compounding. If you read this book with a sincere desire to create wealth, protect the wealth you already have, and plan for your family's future, you will discover more about the accumulation of wealth than anything you've ever learned. I often refer to the science of money as "art" because when Pure Compound Interest takes root and blossoms in your life, it is one of the most beautiful things you will ever experience. How can math and money science be so perfect? Welcome to The Science of Compound Interest!

Let's begin with a story from the book *One Grain of Rice*.

> Long ago in India, a servant led an elephant from a royal storehouse to the palace, carrying two full baskets of rice. A village girl named Rani saw that a trickle of rice was falling from one of the baskets. Quickly she jumped up and walked along beside the elephant, catching the falling rice in her skirt. She was clever, and she began to make a plan.
>
> At the palace, a guard cried, "Halt, thief! Where are you going with that rice?"
>
> "I am not a thief," Rani replied. "This rice fell from one of the baskets, and I am returning it now to the Raja."
>
> When the Raja heard about Rani's good deed, he asked his ministers to bring her before him.
>
> "I wish to reward you for returning what belongs to me," the Raja said to Rani. "Ask me for anything, and you shall have it."
>
> "Your highness," said Rani, "I do not deserve any reward at all. But if you wish, you may give me one grain of rice."
>
> "Only one grain of rice?" The Raja exclaimed. "Surely you will allow me to reward you more plentifully, as a Raja should."
>
> "Very well," said Rani. "If it pleased Your Highness, you may reward me in this way. Today, you will give me a single grain of rice. Then, each day for thirty days, you will give me double the rice you gave me the day before. Thus, tomorrow you will give me two grains of rice, the next day four grains of rice, and so on for thirty days."
>
> "This seems to be a modest reward," said the Raja. "But you shall have it."

And Rani was presented with a single grain of rice.

The next day, Rani was presented with two grains of rice.

And the following day, Rani was presented with four grains of rice.

On the 9th day, Rani was presented with 256 grains of rice. She had received in all 511 grains of rice, enough for only a small handful. "This girl is honest, but not very clever," thought the Raja. "She would have gained more rice by keeping what fell into her skirt!"

On the 12th day, Rani received 2048 grains of rice, about four handfuls.

On the 13th day, she received 4096 grains of rice, enough to fill a bowl.

On the 16th day, Rani was presented with a bag containing 32,768 grains of rice. All together she had enough rice for two bags. "This doubling up adds up to more rice than I expected" thought the Raja. "But surely her reward won't amount to much more."

On the 20th day, Rani was presented with sixteen more bags filled with rice.

On the 21st day, she received 1,048,576 grains of rice, enough to fill a basket.

On the 24th day, Rani was presented with 8,388,608 grains of rice — enough to fill eight baskets, which were carried to her by eight royal deer.

On the 27th day, 32 brahma bulls were needed to deliver 64 baskets of rice. The raja was deeply troubled. "One grain of rice

> has grown very great indeed," he thought. "But I shall fulfill the reward to the end, as a Raja should."
>
> On the 29th day, Rani was presented with the contents of two royal storehouses.
>
> On the 30th and final day, 256 elephants crossed the province, carrying the contents of the last four royal storehouses—536,870,912 grains of rice.
>
> Altogether, Rani had received more than one billion grains of rice. The Raja had no more rice to give. "And what will you do with this rice," said the Raja with a sigh, "now that I have none?"
>
> "I shall give it to all the hungry people," said Rani, "and I shall leave a basket of rice for you, too, if you promise from now on to take only as much rice as you need."

More than one billion grains of rice had stemmed from a single decision to begin compounding! This one powerful decision started a sequence of events that would successfully achieve the phenomenon of Exponential Growth, the principle of unlimited wealth potential.

To understand how this is possible, I want to introduce to you my growth theory I call a "Compound Cycle."

A Compound Cycle is the natural energy and time it takes for something to double in size. From 1 to 2, 2 to 4, 4 to 8, and so on. Each cycle usually requires a similar amount of time and energy; however, as cycles mature and compound on each other, the duration of each cycle may be the same, but the outcome is magnified, eventually becoming exponential. In the first cycle from 1 to 2 grains of rice, the net increase is one. To achieve that first cycle, or 1 grain of rice increase, required a certain amount of energy and time. By day 30 (the 29th Compound Cycle), that same amount of energy and time produced a cycle worth 268,435,456 grains of rice. This is the power and effect of the next cycle!

After 29 Compound Cycles, a single item has the potential to grow to more than 530,000,000 times its original value. Translated to money, $1 has the potential to grow by itself to $536,870,912 with no additional investment or energy by the individual. The only requirement is COMPOUNDING over TIME! Pause for a moment and consider how this could apply to your life. With a little investment and enough time for that investment to grow, the power of compounding can produce significant financial abundance for anyone, anywhere, of any income level.

COMPOUND CYCLES

COMPOUND CYCLE	INVESTMENT	COMPOUND GROWTH	ACCOUNT VALUE
START	$1	-	$1
1	-	$1	$2
2	-	$2	$4
3	-	$4	$8
4	-	$8	$16
5	-	$16	$32
6	-	$32	$64
7	-	$64	$128
8	-	$128	$256
9	-	$256	$512
10	-	$512	$1,024
11	-	$1,024	$2048
12	-	$2,048	$4096
13	-	$4,096	$8,192
14	-	$8,192	$16,384
15	-	$16,384	$32,768
16	-	$32,768	$65,536
17	-	$65,536	$131,072
18	-	$131,072	$262,144
19	-	$262,144	$524,288
20	-	$524,288	$1,048,576
21	-	$1,048,576	$2,097,152
22	-	$2,097,152	$4,194,304
23	-	$4,194,304	$8,388,608
24	-	$8,388,608	$16,777,216
25	-	$16,777,216	$33,554,432
26	-	$33,554,432	$67,108,864
27	-	$67,108,864	$134,217,728
28	-	$134,217,728	$268,435,456
29	$1	$268,435,456	$536,870,912

What the story of one grain of rice reveals is the established, mathematical road-map to wealth, wealth that you can achieve once you understand what pure compounding is, how it works, and what it takes to achieve it, and then dedicate some resources to making it happen as soon as possible. Unfortunately, this knowledge has been lost. To make matters worse, it is in direct conflict with what we were taught at home, in school, and by society regarding money.

Bits and pieces of this truth find their way into various memes on Instagram, Facebook and other social media platforms, not to mention financial influencers attempting to build empires on partial truths; these fragments evoke a dopamine rush when we put them into practice. Unfortunately, hundreds of financial investment plans are either outdated, incomplete, or both due to a lack of understanding the fundamental principles of compounding.

Therefore, it is my personal mission to demonstrate one COMPLETE solution—a feat that others have deemed impossible. It begins by embracing the true nature and power of Compound Interest and a deep understanding of the concept of *Compound Cycles!* Then, applying this knowledge of the infinite energy of money and its unwavering desire to grow for you!

When Albert Einstein called Compound Interest the greatest mathematical discovery of all time, the most powerful force in the Universe, man's greatest invention, he was not exaggerating. And if he didn't say it (some question if he did), then I am! There is nothing like it.

Throughout this book, I will explain the true nature of Compound Interest in a new, compelling, and factual way that is verifiable, and a way that you likely have never heard before. After years in business hitting home runs and strikeouts, repeatedly, my perspective has become deeply rooted in the belief that consistently protecting your hard-earned money has more long-term value to your wealth than the drive to occasionally win big.

Let's begin with the idea that the rate of return inside an investment is NOT the most consequential aspect in the pursuit of wealth; nor are fees, guarantees, securities, tax advantages, leverage, or even debt. Not any one of these aspects can be said to have the most impact . . . but **ALL OF THEM**

TOGETHER. We likely were taught to treat these concepts as individual focus points. However, success does not depend on any one aspect, rather all combined—each one playing a role in the balanced approach to maximizing Compound Cycles (the period during which money doubles).

The most empowering decision you can make right now is to begin as soon as possible. Delay prevents the compounding from beginning, which means fewer cycles during your lifetime. As you can see from the previous graphic, the later Compound Cycles are when you make the most money. Some may tell themselves that next year is the year they will start their financial plan, yet tomorrow never comes for most, as there will always be a reason to not begin. And because they started their financial plan at 40 years old instead of 20 years old, they missed at least three Compound Cycles (typically taking six to seven years per cycle in a well-designed strategy), a cost of millions of dollars to them and their family's future.

What is amazing about a Compound Cycle is the notion of doubling value during a given period. How do you double your retirement income? You produce an additional Compound Cycle in the same time frame (or start earlier). How do you quadruple your wealth in your lifetime? You achieve two additional Compound Cycles. The mathematics are straightforward as I hold time constant and increase the number of Compound Cycles.

Thinking of a person's lifetime as a *cycle*, starting at 20 years old instead of 40, and producing three more cycles in their lifetime, increases wealth by 800% (2x to 4x to 8x). That's eight times more wealth, using the same investment amount but allowing more time! If a parent opens a compounding account for a child, it has the potential to produce five to six more cycles in their lifetime, which is 16–32x more wealth than will be achieved by someone who waits until the age of 35. It sounds simple, because it is. It's following the simple mathematical rules of Compound Interest.

When I refer to the "Lost Science of Compound Interest," it's more specifically the lost *appreciation* for Compound Cycles. This differentiates my approach from everything you have read or been told. The focus of this book is explaining what achieves a Compound Cycle and how to accelerate it to increase the number of cycles in your lifetime, which will ultimately produce millions of dollars for anyone who wants it.

For example, if you make $30,000 per year, you can produce Compound Cycles in your lifetime that will result in a nest-egg of millions; someone who earns 6- or 7-figure income per year has the potential to build a legacy they never dreamed possible. Know this: It is NOT free! It is an effort that requires time, work, discipline, and belief, and when applied, it will provide tremendous value (and freedom) to those who commit.

To be accountable for my claims, this study will require math and science, as well as examples illustrating how Compound Interest works, what impedes it, what magnifies it, and ultimately, how to maximize it for your benefit. Guard yourself against becoming overwhelmed as you read because it will all make sense as the book breaks down the simple but necessary components of compounding.

There are two reactions that generally follow my thorough explanation: "Why has no one ever told me this?" or "This sounds too good to be true!" As with most discoveries, we've been indoctrinated to believe that what we were taught in the past is the only truth and conditioned to be skeptical when new information is presented that contradicts our current beliefs.

To these reactions, my typical response is always with empathy: Compound Interest is slow, steady, and secure. There are no shortcuts as it requires discipline and is often a little boring. It does NOT require any special deals nor any unique talent and it has no immediate excitement or gratification. It's plain, simple math that requires time to mature. Are you willing to start right now and put in the time? That's the only question you need to ask yourself!

By following the blueprint of this book, your mind and heart will soon open to the belief that you can achieve anything in your life through the phenomenon of compounding. You deserve financial freedom and prosperity. We work hard; we care for our families, and we all want the best future, in pursuing our own dreams. Most people want to be healthy, happy, and safe. Although money doesn't buy happiness, it does buy freedom and flexibility to transform our lives, as well as positively affecting the people and causes we care about. That is the opportunity at hand—the path to freedom!

As with all my writings, videos, and presentations, I invite anyone who wants more information, clarification, or just an open discussion on how Compound Interest can benefit your life, to reach out to me through my email at Curtis@CurtisRay.com, on any social media platform or my website CompoundInterest.com.

Financial freedom, a path rather than a destination, is one of the most important skills you can learn in your life, and I will do everything I can to help you create the opportunity for yourself to achieve the personal wealth and freedom you've dreamed of!

Once again, welcome to the Science of Compound Interest! Let's get started!

"Time is Your Friend; Impulse is Your Enemy. Take Advantage of Compound Interest . . . "

John Bogle

NOTES/THOUGHTS

CHAPTER 2
Everyone Ends Up Poor™

In 2018, having written an Amazon Bestseller titled *Everyone Ends Up Poor*, both praise and hatred rolled in from the tens of thousands of copies sold around the world. The book had been my first attempt at explaining the simple truth that the traditional system has very little potential to produce the wealth we were promised because of one significant reason: it was never focused on the long-term success of Compound Cycles. Rather, the traditional system focuses on various short-term distractions ("shiny objects") that may make us feel good, initially, but cannot deliver consistently.

Financial advisors, social media influencers, insurance agents, debt-free minimalists, and various other gurus claim to have "THE WAY" to provide security, freedom, and wealth in your life. But then something terrible happens . . . you wake up on your 65th birthday, or whenever you retired, and guess what? Low retirement income!

"THE WAY" was merely a fallacy to entice you to use their services. Investment portfolios, life insurance contracts, annuities, real estate rentals, cryptocurrencies, starting a business, and nearly every other investment opportunity leads to one glaring truth—DOWNSIZING! Why? Because the "gurus" never understood the true nature of Compound Interest, and we never checked the math to compare the retirement income WE wanted with the one THEY could deliver.

This fallacy was not done maliciously; most people in finance offer their services to serve the needs of others, sincerely help people, and deliver results. Unfortunately, they have married themselves to a system based on a linear mindset, a simple, outdated "how it has always been done" approach. These systems are based on instant gratification and short-term results: the great feeling of paying off debt, the excitement of hitting a home run investment, deferring taxes for an immediate win, paying the lowest expenses, or just a plain old YOLO (You Only Live Once) mentality.

Nothing is inherently wrong with any of their approaches, as they can provide some positive results, but first and foremost, they were designed to create a quick dopamine response through tangible results in the near future. Regrettably, this rush we are hard-wired to crave has devastating long-term effects, including the inability to produce compounding results, or at least not to their full potential.

Albert Bartlett, a physics professor at the University of Colorado Boulder, stated "the greatest shortcoming of the human race is our inability to understand exponential functions," or in simple terms, our ability to make the best long-term decisions for ourselves. We make linear decisions (helpful in the short-term) because it is how we are wired! We are literally fighting biology.

Let's touch on a few topics quickly that I will address more thoroughly later in the book. These topics will likely open your eyes to the way the mainstream promotes investing for retirement and even how we live our lives. And this stands in stark contrast to the energy of compounding and wealth.

Linear mindset (also called the Natural Man) vs. Exponential mindset have been in conflict since the beginning of time. Do we do what feels best now or do what is best forever? Because a linear mindset offers easy-to-understand instant gratification and typically makes us "feel good" at the moment, it significantly influences our decision making.

Most industries, but the financial services industry specifically, have used nearly all linear concepts to gain clients, make sales, build empires, and get likes on social media, all while leaving nearly everyone else poor. Linear mindset takes no prisoners!

No Risk, No Reward

We have all heard the motto and love it. It's a common phrase among entrepreneurs that most everyone believes without question.

But what would you think if I told you this one philosophy was the sole reason most entrepreneurs end up poor? The idea that you must put yourself at risk in order to receive the reward is one of the most ridiculous ideas that most of us have accepted as fact. We even promote it to our kids and those looking for help because it validates and justifies risky choices that excite us.

In fact, it's a cop-out for the risky decisions we make. Would we ever say "I need to put my marriage at risk to have my best marriage?" Or "I need to put my body at risk to have the best health?" Or "I want the best future for my kids so I will put them at risk?" Of course not! Such irrational ideas make no sense. They represent insanity to its very core.

Why do we believe that slow, steady, and secure is an accepted key to success in every single aspect of our lives besides our money? Because the linear mind, even when disguised as a good long-term decision, can't see past tomorrow.

What is wrong with the concept of *No risk, No reward*? It destroys all the benefits of compounding! Whether that effect is in wealth, health, marriage, or business, the fact remains that risk destroys compounding. Lance Roberts, writer for RIA (Real Investment Advice), in his investing advice series "Everything You Are Being Told About Savings & Investing Is Wrong: Part I" states "the power of compounding only works when you do not lose money."

We consider the stock market to be one of the best, most-exciting investment vehicles for lasting growth; it seems to offer home-run potential around every corner. The potential of being an early buyer of a company like Amazon is everyone's hope—the proverbial "easy money." But for every investor that happened to pick the "right stock at the right time," there are thousands who did not and never will! Like home runs and strikeouts, ups and downs are commonplace in the stock market. We take significant risk for the unlikely probability of a huge reward. Over time, it seems nearly impossible to pick enough winners, while avoiding the losers, to achieve significant results when choosing individual stocks.

In 1975, this conundrum was the inspiration for John Bogle, founder of Vanguard, to completely change the way we invest in the stock market with the advent of the Index Fund; a collection of the largest companies rolled into one mutual fund, enabling investors to bet on the collective market rather than individual companies. By so doing, Bogle's approach sought to produce a positive result for the investor more regularly, hold expenses to a minimum, and reduce the risk of strikeouts. This approach to diversification would transform and evolve investments because it was based on slow-and-steady rather than hoping for the home run at the risk of a strikeout.

Money managers and stockbrokers ridiculed Bogle for being content with the "average," but can you guess what has happened since 1975? Science and math won! It always does. Up to 80% of the time, an index fund beats the average returns of stock pickers. 80%! Slow-and-steady, taking the collective approach, produced better results for the investor and accomplished this with significant savings in management fees.

So why would an individual investor ever use a stock trader or money manager? That dang linear mind! The biological intruder arrives as expected to convince us that without risk we will receive no reward; that our money manager is better than an index fund because he or she is picking stocks that will outperform, and, theoretically, earn us more than the average! Maybe one of their picks will even hit the grand slam that makes us rich! Reality (and data) says that it rarely turns out that way. Worse, when we *do* win big, we also get bit by the gambler's ruin, putting our earnings at greater risk only to rarely, if ever, hit it big again.

There is no disputing the fact that John Bogle was a pioneer; however, he was also missing one crucial part of the success equation. He didn't fully appreciate just how detrimental risk is in destroying compounding effects. From 1975 to 1999, the US stock market returns were incredible. With relatively few down markets in that time frame, investors failed to consider risk to be an important part of the equation. Then came the monumental shock with the tech bust, followed, eight years later, by the Great Recession.

CHAPTER 2   EVERYONE ENDS UP POOR™   15

The 21st century changed the game! Risk and its consequences became commonplace. So just how bad is risk in any form, even in an index fund that beats money managers up to 80% of the time?

Let's look at the performance of the S&P 500 over the period 2000–2012—thirteen full years. What value did it deliver for an investor? On Jan 1, 2000, the value of the S&P 500 was 1,425.59. Over the ensuing thirteen years, all manner of outcomes occurred: home runs, strikeouts, singles, doubles, grand slams and everything in between. Dotcom crushed us, 2003 rebounded, 2008 bubble bust, 2009 rebounded and various other ups and downs. And where did the S&P 500 land on Jan 1, 2013? It was 1,480.40, which is zero growth in 13 years!

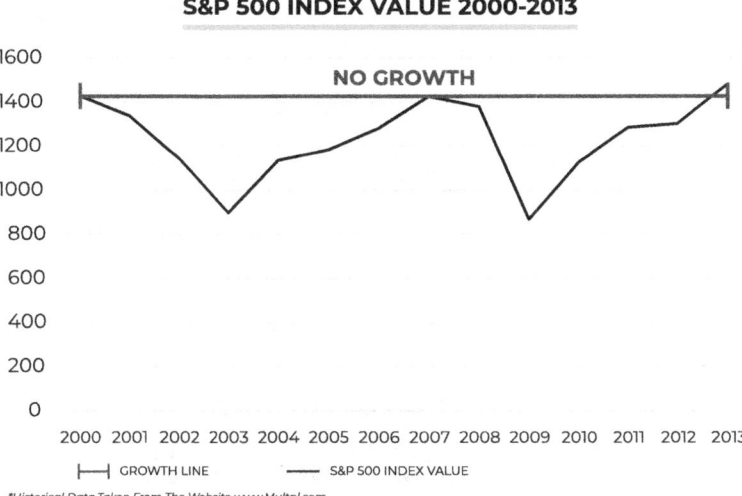

Thankfully, that is not the entire story as that number does not include dividends received, meaning at least your wealth maintained its value relative to inflation—it just had NO growth. Your Advisor likely assured you that after his recommendations lost your money, if you stayed the course, you would get it back. The facts: In 2000–2002, his recommendations lost nearly half your money, then 2003–2007 was totally kicking butt and got it all back. In 2008, you lost nearly half your money again, but from 2009 to 2012 it then came roaring back!

Why is this so important? The market rebounded, right? That's the advisors' guidance, adding that the market will always rebound, so just be patient? Which is true, but at what cost? We lost thirteen years of potential growth equating to roughly two Compound Cycles! And what are two Compound Cycles worth to your future self? MILLIONS! The decision you made in 1999 (or make today) could cost you millions of dollars over the next 50 years.

Let me illustrate just how destructive risk really is and why the mindset of "it will always rebound" will cost millions to your future self.

To illustrate, let's assume your 401(k) account value in 2000 was $100,000. Yes, you will continue to add to it but let's look at what happens to the balance of $100,000 you had January 1st, 2000 invested in a risk-based platform such as the S&P 500 Index Fund. This could also be mutual funds, stocks, real estate, and various other mainstream, risk-based investments. Here is the comparison illustrating the impact of risk:

RISK-BASED COMPOUND CYCLES

YEAR	ACCOUNT VALUE
2000	$100,000
2007	$100,000
2012	$100,000

SECURE COMPOUND CYCLES

YEAR	ACCOUNT VALUE
2000	$100,000
2007	$200,000
2012	$325,000

*Assuming a Compound Cycle Every 7 Years.

A whopping $225,000 difference attributed to nearly two additional Compound Cycles while the traditional portfolio hit both home runs and strikeouts! This shows the foundational principle that risk kills compounding by erasing the benefit of time.

But was it a $225,000 loss? Not when you understand how compounding works. That loss of two cycles had a much larger impact. Here is what the real potential loss was when one assumes a standard 7-year Compound Cycle over the next 35 years:

RISK-BASED COMPOUND CYCLES

YEAR	ACCOUNT VALUE
2012	$100,000
2019	$200,000
2026	$400,000
2033	$800,000
2040	$1,600,000
2047	$3,200,000

SECURE COMPOUND CYCLES

YEAR	ACCOUNT VALUE
2012	$325,000
2019	$650,000
2026	$1,300,000
2033	$2,600,000
2040	$5,200,000
2047	$10,400,000

*Assuming a Compound Cycle Every 7 Years.

Over an investing lifespan of 48 years, assuming there will never be another market collapse in the next 35 years (an unreasonable assumption, especially when one considers that as I write this book, the COVID-19 virus is decimating the world market, thereby validating the unpredictable nature of risk and the many places it can be found), and producing a cycle every 7 years, the decision you made to invest in risk-based compounding rather than secure-based, could have up to an $7,000,000 effect on your lifetime wealth.

How can this be, given that the returns were nearly identical and the invested amount was the same?

Because security produced two additional cycles. It seemed like a $225,000 mistake back in 2012, but as this plays out, any missed cycle due to loss has catastrophic results as time goes on (this is exponential decay, which we will touch on later). Will we miss another cycle with the 2020 collapse? Time will tell!

Though John Bogle was a pioneer who made significant advances in comprehending how money works, especially regarding the impact of expenses, as well as the power of slow and steady compounding, he had not yet solved for the impact of risk. When exposed to risk, we not only lose money; we lose time. When we lose time, we lose cycles, and cycles have unlimited wealth potential as they play out over the course of our life.

No Risk, No Reward? No, the saying should be "Eliminate Risk, Maximize Your Reward!" Slow, steady, and SECURE. That is the formula to create, maximize, and keep wealth!

The 4% Rule: The Safe Withdrawal Rate

The 4% Rule is the rule-of-thumb in financial planning to determine how much someone can "safely" withdraw from their traditional 401(k) / IRA as retirement income. This rule-of-thumb considers the history of risk-based investing.

When the retirement income calculation is made between you and your advisor, what most new retirees suddenly discover is that the number is low, and therefore requires a lifestyle adjustment (i.e., DOWNSIZING!). The fact that nearly all retirees are forced to downsize their lifestyle is telling; the Golden Years are suddenly about surviving instead of thriving. We have come to accept the 4% rule-of-thumb as a constant when it is one of many enablers of risk-based thinking and the consequences that accompany it.

The major flaw in most retirement plans is not that they don't make money (because they do), it's that they don't produce decent sustainable retirement income. The concepts of money in a nest-egg and decent sustainable retirement income are not synonymous. The retirement plans we've come to trust were NOT designed to produce maximum retirement income, as we now know; they were flawed out of the gate.

Mainstream financial services tend to focus on the size of your nest-egg; their ads ask us "what's your number?" as if the answer is a solution instead of a simple marketing ploy. It feels good to see a big number; however, a big nest egg and a big retirement income are not directly correlated.

What I just said probably confused you. How can a large pot of money not produce a great retirement income?

Because it was never designed to. These solutions were designed backwards: they were constructed on the assumption that risk-based investing was required to assure a reward, making it mathematically impossible to produce decent long-term results. They were designed to produce short-term results that feel good now and would incentivize people to save in their working years, only to ultimately be let down in their retirement years.

I call it the Sprint, Run, Jog, Walk method of investing. Exactly the opposite of how Compound Interest works, which is jog, run, and then sprint. One feels good today; the other feels good when it matters.

Imagine running a race in which you begin by sprinting as hard as you can! You are young, it's exciting, and you can handle the pace for a while even though you know you will eventually fatigue. Because it is a marathon, you have plenty of time and can stop and recover as needed. Then, by the middle of the marathon, your energy is diminishing. Your sprint turns into a solid run, then to a solid jog, while requiring a little more recovery time. It doesn't feel so good anymore. By the time you get to the last few miles of the race, you can muster only enough energy to walk. Finally, you limp across the finish line only to be told the real race is just beginning... RETIREMENT!

Everything you did during this marathon was to prepare you for the real race—the next 25–30 years of your life when you can't run anymore. Because you limped across the finish line due to poor planning (which had excited you when you started), you will never recover. This is the reality of the 4% Rule, the expected standard results inside of the risk-based investments of the financial services world: 401(k), 403(b), IRA, Roth IRA, Index Funds, and others.

What many financial advisors fail to recognize and, consequently, fail to discuss with their clients is that however fast you are running (speed representing how much Compound Interest you are making on your investment), the day you cross the finish line to start retirement will determine your retirement income for life. Because of an inefficient race plan sold as an exciting "home run" potential 30 years ago, you are now bound to walking slowly in retirement. This is the consequence of linear thinking, thinking that can produce immediate wins, but poor long-term results. Because of this design, the 4% Rule was created to justify such ineffective and inefficient plans.

Does that sound like the best way to produce the future you dream of, or would a better plan be to start the race with a solid, secure, sustainable pace? A pace that minimizes fatigue, then gradually increases your speed over time, and prepares you to sprint at the end for the win? Jog, Run, Sprint sounds a lot like the scenario created by Compound Interest—exactly opposite of how traditional retirement planning is designed today. Although Compound Interest is not as exciting, it optimizes the compounding effects of money.

Where does the 4% Rule come from?

Here is the math behind it: In a traditional 401(k)/IRA, when you are younger, say during your 20-40s, it is advisable to be a little more aggressive with your investment allocation (sprint the race) and strive for home runs, because there is time to recover from any strikeouts. "The Market will always rebound!" Over time, this method potentially earns a rate of return of 8–12%, which is good. It also comes with risk.

As you get a little older, say into your 50s, the conventional wisdom of our financial advisors is to taper off a little, become more conservative with the allocation of your investments, and favor those producing around a 6–8% rate of return.

Then, as you approach retirement, taper off yet again, into an allocation yielding around 4–6%.

When retirement finally arrives, and you begin to "walk" the race, you need to increase security, so your portfolio produces a return averaging 3–5%.

Each stage is achieved by converting a portion of your stock holdings into more conservative investments, generally bonds.

SPRINT, RUN, JOG, WALK OF INVESTING

AGE	RATE OF RETURN	METHOD
UNDER 40	8-12%	SPRINT
50'S	6-8%	RUN
60'S	4-6%	JOG
RETIREMENT	3-5%	WALK

To maintain your account balance and produce a secure retirement income, they advise you to withdraw only the growth of the account (now a meager 3–5%). The accepted "safe" withdrawal rate is 4%, which is the average return of a conservative portfolio and, not coincidentally, the amount that is systematically replenished. Retirement income depends on your portfolio's ability to replenish what you withdraw.

The size of your account value and the amount of spendable retirement income are not directly correlated. That is the big secret about a great retirement. It is not about how much you have but what is being done with what you have. That might sound odd, but a large nest egg producing low interest produces low retirement income! The focus is all backwards. Everyone (except the super wealthy) will, of necessity, need to downsize because no matter how much is in your 401(k)/IRA, 4% of it is likely not enough to sustain your current lifestyle. To test the math, divide your current income by 0.04, and that is the size of your required nest-egg (if you earn $100,000 that would mean you need $2,500,000 at retirement).

This is why hundreds of websites coach you on how to downsize in retirement because nearly every linear-focused retirement plan fails to produce a good income.

The elusive $1,000,000 portfolio as a retirement nest-egg will safely generate around $40,000 of (taxable) annual income. Even if you had $2,000,000 in your nest egg (rarely achieved), you have a "safe" withdrawal amount of $80,000 (taxable). Approximately 1% of people ever save $1,000,000 or more in their nest-egg; the national average is closer to $200,000 at 65 years old ($8,000 retirement income from that nest-egg).

Ask your Financial Advisor to generate an estimated retirement income report for your portfolio at your desired retirement age (and deduct projected Social Security payments because many reports include Social Security in the retirement income generated from your nest-egg, which it is not!). Unfortunately, you will see the truth about the 4% Rule.

401(k)/IRA NEST EGG	RETIREMENT INCOME
$250,000	$10,000
$500,000	$20,000
$1,000,000	$40,000
$2,000,000	$80,000

*Pre-Tax Retirement Income Inside 401(k)/IRA.

Deferring Your Taxes

It sounds like such a great concept, right? You have the opportunity to pay less in taxes today. Who wouldn't want that?

Not so fast! Deferring your taxes is the financial strategy dependent on an IRS tax-code allowing you to either deduct retirement contributions on your income taxes today or contribute to your employer-sponsored plan with pre-tax dollars. You then pay taxes in the future as you withdraw from your nest-egg. We refer to this deferred system as "qualified money" and this is part of the traditional 401(k) and IRA.

There is an ongoing debate as to the benefit of deferring your taxes, and it has a lot of moving parts. It is important to understand what is best for you. Arm yourself with the facts regarding taxes in order to make the best long-term decisions for your specific circumstances.

Consider that by deferring taxes, you make an agreement with the US government that for a small immediate tax incentive (a feel good), but in return, you have given them the right to not only tax your money and all the growth of your money, but to do so at ANY rate they deem desirable in the future. They have a lien on your nest-egg inside the 401(k)/ IRA of an undetermined future tax amount. Whatever rate Congress determines is in effect when you withdraw from your nest egg is what you must pay. That is why planning for this type of structure is so risky—we cannot be certain how much the "future determined tax rate" of your nest-egg will truly entail.

The other day, someone made a comment to me that was interesting. He said, "you want to know why the government does not worry about the $22 trillion-dollar national debt? They have full access to $26 trillion of taxable assets inside 401(k)s and IRAs!"

A great financial plan has the obligation to, and is, indeed, the essence of, the client's best-interest; to eliminate as many unknowns, mitigate risks, and improve the probability of success on behalf of your future self.

Why would the financial world promote such a concept given the inherent risk?

Most financial advisors promote the deferred system because there is a small immediate win on taxes. It's biology. The instant gratification, once again, is a "feel good" or linear thought process.

They also suggest that this enables you to invest a larger amount of money, which will then compound faster, making you more money.

Let's analyze and validate that claim:

The first myth to debunk is the idea that *more* money compounds faster. When comparing apples to apples, including taxes, this is not true, regardless of what most advisors say.

For example, if you invested $10,000 a year while deferring your taxes at an 8% growth rate and allowed it to compound for 30 years, you would have around $1,100,000 in your account. If you were then taxed 20% on the total account value, you would have $880,000.

Consider the same scenario but use investments upon which you've already paid taxes, such as a Roth account: Taking the same $10,000 a year but taxing the income now at 20%, investing only $8000 a year, then using the same 8% growth rate for the same 30 years, guess what the NET result is? It is the same: $880,000.

The only way to get a different result is to assume different tax rates at either end of that equation; you have no way to know if the future rate will be higher, lower, or the same.

PRE-TAX VS POST-TAX

PRE-TAX INVESTMENT	GROWTH	NEST EGG	INCOME TAX RATE	TOTAL VALUE AFTER TAX
$10,000	8%	$1,100,000	20%	$880,000
POST-TAX INVESTMENT	GROWTH	NEST EGG	INCOME TAX RATE	TOTAL VALUE AFTER TAX
$8,000	8%	$880,000	20%	$880,000

*Assuming the Same Tax Rate in Retirement.

However, the financial world will tell you to defer your tax because you "should" be in a lower tax bracket when you get older. Think about that message; they are already predicting you will be poor (low-income) in retirement. That's the unfortunate assumption of current financial planning!

The 401(k) and IRA are so bad at producing retirement income, by deferring your taxes now, and because your income will be so low in retirement using the 4% Rule, you will naturally be in a lower marginal bracket. That is the very definition of the scarcity mindset!

Having debunked the myth that deferring taxes makes "more" money, consider what is actually true: by deferring taxes to give yourself more to invest in your portfolio, with an asset-based fee—typically around 1% of your account value—your advisor is collecting more fees than he would otherwise.

PRE-TAX CONTRIBUTION FEES

AGE	ANNUAL INVESTMENT	GROWTH	ACCOUNT VALUE	1% ANNUAL FEE	CUMULATIVE FEES
25			$11,000	$110	$110
30			$82,757	$828	$2,689
35		10%	$193,163	$1,932	$9,950
40			$363,037	$3,630	$24,412
45	$10,000		$624,410	$6,244	$49,956
50			$1,007,730	$10,077	$92,362
55		8%	$1,475,501	$14,755	$156,150
60		6%	$2,091,734	$20,917	$248,323
65		4%	$2,676,249	$26,762	**$370,864**

POST-TAX CONTRIBUTION FEES

AGE	ANNUAL INVESTMENT	GROWTH	ACCOUNT VALUE	1% ANNUAL FEE	CUMULATIVE FEES
25			$8,800	$88	$880
30			$66,205	$662	$2,152
35		10%	$154,531	$1,545	$19,530
40			$290,430	$2,902	$39,965
45	$8,000		$499,528	$4,995	$49,956
50			$806,184	$8,062	$73,890
55		8%	$1,180,401	$11,804	$124,920
60		6%	$1,673,404	$16,734	$198,659
65		4%	$2,141,066	$21,411	**$296,694**

*1% Management Fee Used In This Fee Projection.

Let's look at the same numbers more closely (see the following two graphics). The deferred account has a contribution of $10,000 and the post-tax account, $8,000, which is 20% less (our assumed tax rate).

How does this affect the rest of the results? The deferred account generates exactly 20% more in additional pay for the advisor. In this example, it will pay him up to $74,000 more, adding risk to your future self and producing no additional increase in retirement income. How can that design be in your best interest?

PRE-TAX VS POST-TAX FEES

	AGE	AFTER-TAX ANNUAL INCOME	MANAGEMENT FEE
PRE-TAX	65	**$85,640**	$370,864
POST-TAX	65	**$85,640**	$296,694
DIFFERENCE	-	$0	**$74,170**

*4% Retirement Income Used To Determine Projected Income. *For Account Value Projections, See Diagrams Above.

The notion that government and financial services heavily promote one extremely flawed, deferred tax strategy above the rest should tell you something. Deferring taxes does produce many gains: increased profits, increased tax advantages, and increased long-term security. Unfortunately, none of those are working for you!

Compounding Fees

The most powerful quote about the impact of Compound Interest says it "is the 8th wonder of the world, he who understands it, earns it, **he who doesn't, pays it.**"

I rarely include the second half of the quote, as there is no scenario I can think of to illustrate compounding liabilities. Although it is incorrect to think debt is compounding; it is not. Because debt requires minimum payments that are a path to payoff, it is simple interest. Debt increases only if you incur more debt, however, the debt itself does not internally compound on its own. This quote made little sense to me when used regarding debt and other liabilities.

After thoughtful consideration and a search for any liability exhibiting the act of compounding to satisfy this quote, I discovered one in plain sight: the AUM (assets under management) fees inside of traditional financial planning, for which an advisor or firm calculates a percentage of the account value as their payment (expressed as an annual percentage that you are charged quarterly).

How astonishing that the industry that quotes this motto is, in truth, the offender of compounding liabilities. They are the proverbial pot calling the kettle black by demonizing banks and credit card companies (not that either of those earn a pass, but they are at least simple-interest liabilities) while drawing attention away from what is truly going on with your hard-earned money. The ones who control the "compounding system" are also the same who capitalize on it! "He who understands it, earns it, **he who doesn't, pays it**" now makes a lot more sense as a powerful warning.

We love the effect of compounding when it applies to our investments, but have you calculated the effect that compounding has on the fees you are paying? Math is consistent whether it applies to money we make or money we pay.

In the traditional 401(k), according to SmartAssets.com, the national average fee is 2.22% (management fees, trading fees, platform fees, etc.). Meaning that for every $100,000 of YOUR hard-earned savings, the advisor (and firm) is charging $2,220 per year for their guidance and services. Additional details every individual should know:

1. As illustrated in "PRE-TAX VS POST-TAX FEES" Graphic, fees charged to your account value are compounding fees. The total amount you must pay grows as time goes on. Compound Interest is money you receive added to your total value that then earns more interest on the now larger amount. Inside of the traditional system, compounding fees have the same result. As your money grows, the percentage you pay may stay the same, but as Compound Cycles are achieved, you are now paying your advisor double (or triple or quadruple) for his guidance. The fees continue to double each time a cycle is achieved. Has the quality of the guidance doubled? Has the service doubled? Is there a ceiling to how valuable you find the advice? Compounding fees will eventually cost you hundreds of thousands of dollars (or more) over the life of your financial plan. Here are the compounding

fees again but continued through age 90 and reducing the fee to 0.5% in retirement years.

PRE-TAX CONTRIBUTION FEES

AGE	GROWTH	ANNUAL RETIREMENT INCOME	MANAGEMENT FEE	CUMULATIVE FEES
25	10%	NA	1%	$110
30				$2,689
35				$9,950
40				$24,412
45				$49,956
50	8%			$92,362
55				$156,150
60	6%			$248,323
65				$370,864
70				$436,022
75				$496,778
80	4%	$85,640	.5%	$549,655
85				$590,105
90				**$612,233**

*4% Retirement Income Used To Determine Projected Income With a 20% Income Tax Rate. *Assumes Contributions Stop at 65 Years Old. *Retirement Income Increases 3% per Year for Inflation.

2. Fees inside the traditional system are charged whether they make you money or not. In 2008, after the average portfolio lost up to 40% of its value, they still charged the management fee to your account. Whether you win or lose, *they* always win, though they will claim their income was *reduced*. In fact, they may even claim they are sharing in your pain because their income decreased in lockstep with your portfolio value. The truth of the matter is that you lost thousands (or more) while they **made** thousands.

3. Even a low-cost index fund, because it, too, is based on compounding fees, will cost a tremendous amount of money. Using the same investment scenario as above but with an *all-in* expense of 0.25%, the total fees exceed $266,000 in your lifetime.

Hearing "low fees" is a delightful "feel good" moment; however, since compounding is "the most powerful force in the universe," even the smallest fee that is defined as a percentage of a compounding value grows to substantial amounts with the power of time. Compounding can have the greatest influence on your future wealth and freedom, whether for good or bad. Basic understanding allows you to make decisions that maximize the positive compounding (interest) and avoid the negative compounding (fees). Doing both simultaneously will speed up your compounding effect!

Everyone Ends Up Poor! is not just a saying I created. These examples merely scratch the surface of linear concepts that have been sold to us as our best path to freedom. It results from cause and effect, the sequence of events stemming from our acceptance of the status quo rather than the true nature of Compound Interest and its remarkable potential!

> *"If you have not acquired more than a bare existence since your youth, it is because you either have failed to learn the laws that govern the building of wealth, or else you do not observe them."*
>
> **George Clason**

NOTES/THOUGHTS

CHAPTER 3
Yin and Yang

Yin and Yang is *"the concept of dualism describing how seemingly opposite and contrary forces may actually be complementary, interconnected, and interdependent in the natural world, and how they may give rise to each other as they interrelate to one another."* (Wikipedia contributors. "Yin and yang." Wikipedia, The Free Encyclopedia. Wikipedia, The Free Encyclopedia, 5 Feb. 2020.)

Having been born in 1981, I am what some consider a "Xennial" or a member of the age group between Generation X and Millennials. We are the generation who played outside until the streetlights came on and embraced change, including technology, with relative ease. My childhood was 100% analog while my adulthood is now 100% digital. Why is this important? A perfect example of Yin and Yang! Combining the best of both worlds gives me a unique perspective on traditional values that coexist with societal evolution.

Tradition and discipline were ingrained in me throughout my childhood as a result of having been born into the Church of Jesus Christ of Latter-day Saints, but in my case, these concepts were endowed with a small twist. My father, one of the most free-spirited and honest men ever to walk this earth, has a unique outlook on how to follow the rules of society. He taught me they are merely suggestions that I should subject to interpretation under my core values. My moral compass has priority over "rules."

This free-spirited, self-accountable way of living has always been part of my life with the effect of respecting that which was earned and ignoring the noise. Another instance of Yin and Yang! The coexistence of the best of both worlds, always led by my own moral compass instead of conforming to the definition of right and wrong prescribed by others.

I've never had a real job. Aside from quick-money summer jobs with my dad as a teenager. Those summer jobs were the extent of my working career until I started my first business in 2004. As a three-sport athlete in high school while maintaining a 4.2 GPA, work ethic has always been a focus of my upbringing.

In my life, winning has been limited only by the work I was willing to put in. After high school, I served a 2-year religious mission in Santiago, Chile. Upon finishing my mission, I walked onto the Arizona State Wrestling team and earned a scholarship.

While still in college and maintaining a 4.0 GPA, I started my first business in the field of granite countertops—the first source of real income in my life. The business grew quickly and produced more than $1,000,000 in revenue its first year.

As if that didn't keep me busy enough, Erin and I married and began our family; the first of our now five children arrived in 2005. Profound life lessons were the natural result of taking on the stresses, burdens, successes, and responsibility of business and family while being a collegiate athlete.

Yin and Yang! Not only did I take care of myself, maintain the intense edge of competition, and aggressively grow my business in the competitive field of home remodeling. I also provided security and stability for my wife and future children, as well as employees and their families that relied on my business for their income. I learned, in real time, to balance my internal desire to take risks, compete, and win every situation possible with the commitment to a growing family and a team of employees. I became a conservative risk-taker!

You're probably asking yourself, what is a conservative risk-taker? A conservative risk-taker is someone who respects the essential role of security and conservatism, but who is never content with the status quo and is always in pursuit of being better.

Here are the three influences that would ultimately pave the way for the birth of MPI™ in 2014, the first conservative risk-taking financial plan. (Before explaining what MPI™ is, it's important for you to know the influential backstory leading up to 2014).

In my life, I've been blessed with many experiences, perspectives, and opportunities. I grew up in a family of 11, steeped in both the benefits and challenges of a large family dynamic. I learned loyalty, strength, how to fight, how to share, how to serve, how to compete, and other lessons that came from being part of a larger family.

Each of my family members is different but complementary; they each had a hand in shaping who I am today. These influences include but are not limited to:

RAY FAMILY INFLUENCES	
DAD	NEVER FEAR ANYONE OR ANYTHING
MOM	ALWAYS SHOW PEOPLE THEY ARE IMPORTANT
ANITA	GET ALL THE INFORMATION BEFORE YOU MAKE A DECISION
DANNY	ALWAYS PROTECT THOSE WHO NEED PROTECTING
MELISSA	BE AVAILABLE FOR THOSE IN NEED
RUSSELL	SELF-CONFIDENCE
CLINT	SERVE OTHERS
JACOB	HARD WORK IS NEEDED TO ACCOMPLISH ANYTHING
MARCUS	NOTHING IS IMPOSSIBLE
BRETT	BE A GOOD PERSON AND IT WILL ALL WORK OUT

Through my dad's example, I feared nothing about business. I went all-in, never doubting whether or not I would make it. As a natural-born risk-taker, I love the excitement of home run investing, going for the big opportunity, believing I could compete with the best of them, and always being ready for the next big thing.

Within my first 10 years out of college, I started or invested in more than a dozen businesses. Each business seemed like a great opportunity, had a robust forecast, and a solid business plan. Each time I invested, it felt so good, because I did my due diligence, fact-checked the business model, saw the potential, and believed in the business I was investing in.

The excitement of investing in startups is like few feelings that exist—it represents a tremendous potential return to an early investor. Those who are entrepreneurs know what I'm referring to.

I also invested in stocks, an IRA, real estate properties, and a Variable Universal Life Insurance policy. Each one had a value proposition that seemed to fit my financial goals.

All these endeavors seemed like what I was supposed to be doing as I continued to grow wealth, following the advice from those spouting conventional wisdom. I had little debt, paid expenses in cash, invested heavily, and started my own businesses. The result? Home runs and strikeouts. Excitement and frustration. A lot of money and well . . . not so much!

Why did this vicious cycle of winning and losing become a major part of my life? Because I did not understand the universal force of Yin and Yang in business and wealth, the opposite powers that produce beautiful harmony by optimizing the strength of each other. Security and Risk-taking!

Why do I tell you this? What I'm about to explain is the essential foundation of how to optimize Pure Compound Interest and achieve maximum Compound Cycles in your life.

Remember, achieving even one additional Compound Cycle doubles your total wealth. What if you could add two, three, or four additional cycles in your investing lifetime? Understanding that this is possible will be the most important financial insight in this book, having an impact upon your life beyond measure. It is a lesson so powerful that it can provide financial security to anyone, at any income level, who will apply the first Rule of Money... "Pay Yourself First" (save money you earn).

No one has ever attempted to explain this before, but I'm confident by the end of this book, you will have the facts necessary to achieve Pure Compound Interest, the Yin and Yang of Wealth!

They say opposites attract, but do they really? This is where my story gets interesting! After a decade of growing businesses, investing in the next hot thing, and following guidance from experts in their fields, I found myself with a net worth in the millions. Life was great! My business was outperforming all expectations, but because millionaires come and go with every market turn, financial Armageddon would soon catch up to me in 2014. I thought I was above the reach of a downturn, that I knew enough, and that I could outwork anything (or anyone) that would come my way. However, it all came crashing down in the same way it has for millions of other entrepreneurs, executives, and other hard-working people like you and me. Even the billionaires list is a revolving door of people who regularly come and go. None are immune to the devastating effects of risk and loss in investing.

This led me to ask myself, "Is there a better way? Why is money so easy to make, but so difficult to keep?" Then one day, my brother and I found the answer.

This answer was no ordinary "get rich quick" or "secret to investing" answer of the kind that we are bombarded with 24/7 on Social Media, MLMs, or friends pitching their great idea. Nor was the answer "I just need to make more money," which I had told myself for years. It was shockingly simple.

It had always been right in front of me, but I never understood it because of the crippling, linear, mental influence certain words have had, influences that marketing experts and businesses have been exploiting to manipulate our investing habits for decades. These words and phrases include "become a millionaire," "no risk, no reward," "be your own boss," "guaranteed," "lowest cost," and other words known to invoke an emotional reaction.

Every pitch was glaringly one-sided and had a questionable foundation: "become rich," "guaranteed returns," "security," or "financial freedom."

Absent was the combination of Yin and Yang required to optimize the strength of these strategies.

As a seasoned investor, my approach was predominantly aggressive while minimizing risk whenever possible; in other words, striving to do what most investors were and are still doing. We avoid investing in the stupid, but sometimes we strike out.

Risk had never scared me because of my track record of choosing good investments. Ask any investor and we will tell you: we all buy the best stocks, the good flips, the best deals, etc. (said in a sarcastic voice)! But when my "best" investments turned out not to be the "best," I would regroup, lick my wounds, and climb back into the security camp claiming "I will never fall for that again." Of course, as investors, we never tell people about the strikeouts, and often, we fall right back into risk-based investing again!

For me, this cycle repeated itself many times, growing my wealth slowly; nevertheless, my sought-after sense of control and the feeling of financial security seemed just out of reach.

Then the moment of clarity came! In January 2014, my brother Marcus and I discussed for the first time the concept that true success did not lie solely in securing my assets or hitting home runs with my investments, but in a perfect balance of both! The idea that there was a Yin and Yang with respect to money, would change the entire world of investing forever, if it could be implemented. We would become the world's first conservative risk-takers in the realm of financial planning!

This concept resonated with my risk-averse side and stimulated my risk-taking sides (Yin and Yang). The notion that both sides were needed to achieve secure sustainable wealth, both working together as dual, balanced forces to achieve the best outcome by protecting oneself from loss while assertively growing wealth.

At first, it made little sense because it sounded too easy. How could you be a conservative risk-taker?

By using the principle of Yin and Yang!

Did I lose you with the thought that you can have both security and risk, simultaneously, to maximize your future? Please continue reading, as I will explain it thoroughly.

How do I know Yin and Yang of Wealth is possible?

Because it is exactly what Einstein was trying to tell us when he said look to Compound Interest, the 8th Wonder of the world, the greatest mathematical discovery of all time!

What is even more amazing is that this can be explained by a simple math equation—a direct and clean blueprint of how to achieve the Yin and Yang of wealth, the purest form of Compound Interest.

We have had it for decades, in plain sight, yet didn't know how to apply it with consistency. Remember when Einstein said, "He who understands it, earns it!" Well, here it is; time to understand what Pure Compound Interest really is:

$$y = a(1 + r)^x$$

The possibility of maximizing conservative risk-taking behavior sounds crazy! I don't deny this. Remember, my brother Marcus doesn't believe in the concept of "impossible." That is his biggest influence on me: limits do not exist.

This mentality sometimes leads to crazy ideas that literally are impossible. But this time, I based it in math and science, with a formula and guidance from Einstein himself! Math cannot be manipulated and has no emotion; therefore, if the math works, it was possible.

When we first began working through various "what if" scenarios, I was prepared to confront the impossible. The concept itself, let alone the application, took me weeks to wrap my head around until one day, it all clicked. It all made sense.

See, conventional advice tells us to diversify some of our money into high growth and some into security and low growth, that both play a role in "diversification" and will produce some result. But these two categories fight each other, rather than building or enhancing each other, and this diminishes their individual strengths while producing underwhelming results.

Once the concept clicked, I became obsessed with learning about Compound Interest and the phenomenon of the Exponential Growth Curve. The more I researched, the more it made sense. As I came to understand, it became clear why it is the "greatest mathematical discovery of all time," "the most powerful force in the Universe," and "greatest invention man has ever produced."

The more I stress-tested the math, the more it was validated. For decades, we have had the blueprint to the most secure path to financial freedom, and not a single financial expert has studied it, explained it, or even tried to achieve it. Why? Because, in the environment of the status quo, it was impossible to produce Exponential Growth without risk!

EXPONENTIAL GROWTH CURVE

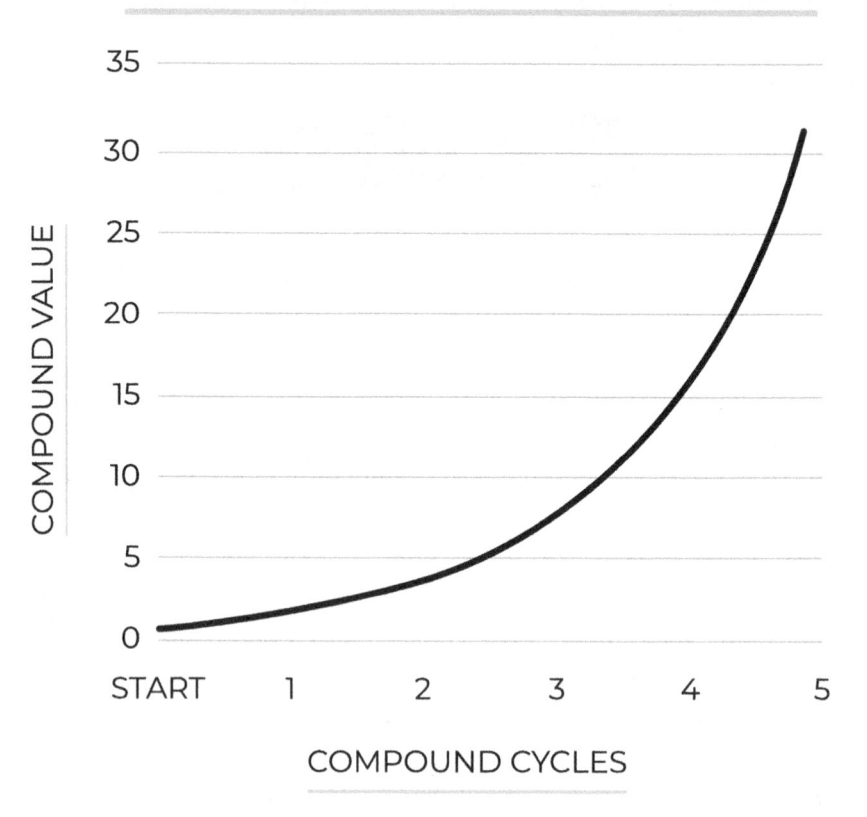

Over the following five years of research, which continues to this day, the reality of Pure Compound Interest and Exponential Growth came to life. Understanding Compound Interest, Compound Cycles, risk, loss, reward, and all that impact this phenomenon was the key to achieving it. No single item was key, but all of them working in unison. We had been doing it wrong by putting too much focus on individual financial concepts while wholly ignoring others.

Exponential Growth requires a revolutionary Yin and Yang approach. Opposite forces working together for optimal results. And how do I know this? Because the equation of wealth explains it. It's right there when we educate ourselves to *see* it:

$$y = a(1 + r)^x$$

There it is: (+) and (r). (+) represents security and conservative action, while (r) designates maximizing growth and risk-taking behavior. Both are coexisting, supporting each other, and ultimately optimizing each other.

What does this all mean?

Opposite forces working together can maximize the potential of your money! Exponential Growth (Pure Compound Interest) is a cause-and-effect relationship, compounding actions, each playing a role in amplifying the power of the component effort. The full equation is in sequential order, step by step. Therefore, if we apply each part of the formula in consecutive order, the result is a given.

What were our findings?

The Yin (Security) and Yang (Growth) of money exists; when the formula is followed, Exponential Growth is the result every single time. A theory that had never been applied in the financial planning world can produce more wealth than any other approach previously attempted. As mentioned, Yin (security) is powerful by herself and Yang (growth) is powerful by himself, but when the two work together, mathematical magic happens.

> *"The Motion of Yin and Yang Generates All Things in Nature"*
>
> **Meh Jiuzhang**

NOTES/THOUGHTS

CHAPTER 4

The Wealth Equation: The Exponential Growth Curve

The Wealth Equation! A formula so perfect, it can take anyone, in any situation, and guide them to prosperity! It's called the Exponential Growth Curve, the formula for achieving Pure Compound Interest!

$$y = a(1 + r)^x$$

COMPOUNDING CONTRIBUTIONS

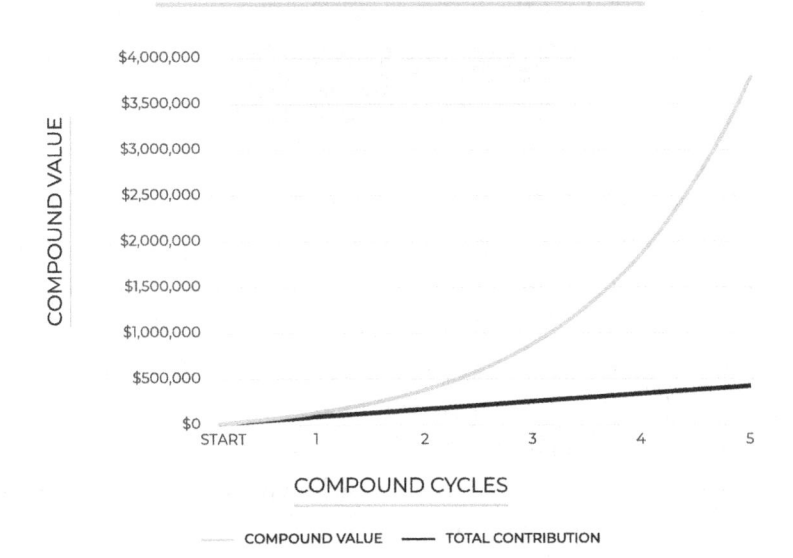

Result Based on a $1,000 Monthly Contribution, and an Assumed 7 Year Compound Cycle.

I define this equation as "a rate becoming more rapid over time, securely!" Doing so securely is key! Exponential Growth, or uninterrupted compounding, is pure growth energy because it accomplishes the rarest of feats: unlimited potential with no risk of losing. When Einstein stated this was the 8th Wonder of the World, he did so because he knew that if it could be achieved in any aspect of life, it would change the world for the better.

In the financial world, most people mistakenly claim traditional risk-based investments are Compound Interest. And although such investments have elements of compounding, they also experience compounding decay, or loss. Pure Compound Interest in finance is continual, positive compounding interest.

Most financial advisors believe this is an impossible scenario, one of theory and philosophy, because of the difficulty to achieve security and optimal growth simultaneously. They are seeing this through the mindset of "No Risk; No Reward."

Before we go any further, let's break down the Wealth Equation theory first to create a foundational understanding for each component. Once we understand each component, this will then allow us to understand how the equation fits together. Understanding also allows us to test, validate, and affirm that the theory works.

$$y = a(1 + r)^x$$

As you can see, there are five components: **a, 1, +, r, x**. What does each mean in plain language and how do we apply them? Many people look at the formula and turn away, assuming it is too complicated, but I promise you, it is very simple to understand when each piece is explained.

To start, we must understand the **(y)**: How it all starts! What do you want out of your life? Are you willing to go after it? **(y)** results from the action you take (or don't take). In a personal financial scenario, **(y)** represents your financial goals and desires.

Now, here are the five components to achieving the financial freedom you seek to do what you want to do, when you want to do it, and with whom you want—FREEDOM!

(a): Your Investment In Your Future Self! It is essential to always Pay Yourself First! This is the amount of effort and money you, as an individual, will put into the equation for your future self. To achieve Pure Compound Interest, (a) must be more than 0, because we know that anything multiplied by zero is ZERO. If you are unwilling to put any money into your personal compounding equation, it will always be 0. To achieve wealth, your efforts and money must go into the equation. The bigger (a) is in the equation, the faster the rest of the equation grows. The NET compounding results are amplified as (a) becomes larger.

(1): Your Commitment! This is the starting point when you ignite the fuse that drives the engine. Start immediately. Any goal you might have, if put off until tomorrow, will probably never happen. Every day you wait delays the maturing of a Compound Cycle.

(+): Your Security! Protect yourself from loss at all costs. Never move backward. I will continue to explain the catastrophic effects of loss throughout the book because I found it is the missing piece in most peoples' wealth equation. Break-even is not a loss and has no negative impact on your wealth equation so the importance of (+) is to never lose! Risk/loss eliminates all possibility of Pure Compound Interest; changing the plus to a negative sign, transforms Exponential Growth into exponential decay.

(r): Your Growth! The maximized growth potential of Compound Interest. This follows security in priority. Without growth, your wealth equation cannot produce Exponential Growth. Growth comes in two forms; maximum rate of return and maximum rate of compounding, which are not the same thing. One gives you the best immediate result while the other gives you the best long-term result. They must be balanced.

(x): Your Acceleration! This represents time, leverage, or both. With enough time, the smallest amount of anything compounding will achieve astonishing results. However, this process could take your entire life to achieve great results, which is where leverage comes into the equation. Leverage is the ability to use other resources, along with your own, to speed up your wealth equation.

If you can use O.P.M. (Other People's Money), an acronym synonymous with borrowing money from a bank or other financial institution, to enhance the (**a**) in the equation, your results can be amplified.

If you can supercharge the amount of effort or money going into your equation (yours plus leverage), this can now achieve Exponential Growth significantly faster because it accelerates the rate of Compound Cycles.

Those are the ingredients to financial freedom. It may appear too simple, but recall that all ingredients must be present and working together (Yin and Yang) for you to achieve 'y.' To summarize; the ingredients required to achieve unlimited wealth through Compound Interest are:

a = Your Investment

1 = Your Commitment

+ = Your Security

r = Your Growth

x = Your Acceleration (Leverage)

What is amazing about this wealth equation is that is does not apply only to money, which is not a surprise given that Einstein spent a lifetime pondering our universe. $Y = a(1 + r)^x$ can apply to any aspect of your life.

Do you want the best marriage? Invest your personal efforts, commit to the goal immediately, secure it by not putting your efforts at risk, grow your efforts, and speed up your efforts through additional resources or continuous time.

You want the best health? Invest your personal efforts, commit to the goal immediately, secure it by not putting your efforts at risk, grow your efforts, and accelerate your efforts through additional resources or continuous time.

Do you want anything in your life? Follow the Wealth Equation as it can take any goal you have from A to Infinite!

There are some great examples of people in society who follow this equation for maximum success. They don't go for home runs, but rather slow, steady, secure progress, always trying to compound their efforts, using every resource available, and always avoiding risk as often as possible. It's not always perfect, but the long-term results are superior to anything else, even when it makes little sense how they are doing it. Who are these people?

Well, anyone who follows me knows there is one person I often reference concerning compounding efforts and maximizing every opportunity available... The G.O.A.T.—The one and only Tom Brady! Is he the most athletic? Does he have the most talent around him? Does he always have the best playing conditions?

No, but you know what he does have? $Y = a(1 + r)^x$ as his blueprint! He puts in his investment (energy), with an unwavering commitment, doesn't put himself at risk or take steps backward, grows his connection with his teammates, studies and trains relentlessly, and uses time and leverage to speed up and enhance the probability of winning.

Why has he been so successful for 20 years, like no one we have ever seen? Because he follows the success equation, never takes steps backward and allows compounding to do its magic! Natural talent is good; compounding is better!

So, what is the reason other investments fail to achieve this powerful force? Time to break down the linear mindset and why it has been holding all of us back.

The Investment Equation

The investment community has taught us our entire life that wealth results from saving inside a 401(k) or IRA with index funds or mutual funds, real estate rentals, cryptocurrencies, business, and various other investments. If that's the case, why do few people ever achieve actual wealth? Let's start with where it all begins, the Investment Equation. The Compound Counterfeit!

$$y = a(1 +/- r)^x$$

Wait! This is the Exponential Growth Equation . . . right? Because Investment Equations can have all the same components, they can be confused with one another; however, there is one glaring difference: the negative sign in the equation, +/- which stands for risk and the possibility of loss. That tiny difference makes a huge impact on your overall success. Loss eliminates or delays the probability of a Compound Cycle(s) or achieving Exponential Growth.

The Investment Equation mathematically explains why what we have been doing cannot produce the full potential of our money. Many people, especially financial advisors and investors, become angry and want to argue the facts. They say, "but Curtis, stocks and investments produce Compound Interest too!" They do, and they can make a lot of money, but they also include Compound Decay, which is a type of loss. When decay is added to the equation, "rebounding" from loss is required, which means taking steps backwards and losing time. We know, from our previous discussion, time is a significant factor in the achievement of wealth! And when you lose time, you lose a potential Compound Cycle, diminishing your wealth exponentially as every ensuing day passes.

Let's continue breaking through that linear mindset. In your pursuit of freedom and wealth, there is one truth about money that you likely haven't heard as a focus: The principle of NOT LOSING your money! This has a greater impact on creating wealth than the thrill of huge investment opportunities. It's not as exciting, but if you want the best long-term results and sustainable income, not losing comes ahead of any *home-run* opportunity.

Why and how can that be? Because with traditional investing, losses have a larger influence on money than gains! In the (+/-) equation, minus is much more influential than the plus, given that we are constrained by time.

Let me explain. If you had invested $10,000 and lost 50% of it because of risk, how much money do you have? $5,000. If one second after you lost 50%, you gained 50% back, or "rebounded," how much money would you have? In most people's minds, you broke even, and the financial world will tell you that you have a 0% average, or **Arithmetic** average. But now you have only $7,500. A 50% loss followed by a 50% gain = −25% ACTUAL return, called a **Geometric** average.

Arithmetic and Geometric averages are not identical regarding money, and they rarely explain this. A 50% loss takes a 100% gain to break even or truly rebound. One step backwards requires TWO steps forward just to get your money back. The time required to restore your money is a lost opportunity for compounding. That's the cause-and-effect impact of the decision to invest with risk present.

ARITHMETIC VS GEOMETRIC RETURNS

MARKET LOSS	MARKET GAIN	ARITHMETIC RETURN (BREAK-EVEN)	GEOMETRIC RETURN (ACTUAL)
-10%	10%	0%	-1%
-20%	20%		-4%
-30%	30%		-9%
-40%	40%		-16%
-50%	50%		-25%

Whenever I speak about achieving Pure Compound Interest, most people, including financial advisors, underestimate the power of "never striking out." Focusing on never losing protects your hard-earned money from the negative impact of risk-based investing. It is YOUR money, not the financial advisors, therefore we must make this a priority. Investments that lose principal value whenever there is a downturn require you to make up that loss.

The finance world says it all the time: Don't worry, the market will rebound, which is true.

However, because time is essential to maximize Compound Interest, loss in investing carries an increased negative effect on your money! Because you lost money, you lost time, because you lost time, you slowed down a Compound Cycle, and because you slowed down your next cycle, your end-result is drastically diminished. It's the cause and effect of the time equation of money and Compound Cycles.

Let's chart the result to visually review the effect of both (+) and (−) on your wealth potential using the S&P 500 Index Fund inside your 401(k) with an all-in assumed expense of 1% (the national average is 2.22%). Assume you started with $100,000 at the end of 1999. Where are the +'s and −'s and what influence do they have on your money?

S&P 500 RETURNS WITH DIVIDENDS

YEAR	S&P 500 RETURNS	ACTUAL CASH
1999	-	$100,000
2000	-9.11%	$89,981
2001	-11.98%	$78,409
2002	-22.27%	$60,338
2003	28.72%	$76,891
2004	10.82%	$84,358
2005	4.79%	$87,515
2006	15.74%	$100,277
2007	5.46%	$104,694
2008	-37.22%	$65,070
2009	27.11%	$81,883
2010	14.87%	$93,119
2011	2.07%	$94,096
2012	15.88%	$107,948
2013	32.43%	$141,526
2014	13.81%	$159,459
2015	1.31%	$159,933
2016	11.93%	$177,223
2017	21.94%	$213,944
2018	-4.42%	$202,443
2019	31.49%	$263,531

*S&P 500, Annual Returns Taken From www.MoneyChimp.com. *1% Management Fee Used.

CHAPTER 4   THE WEALTH EQUATION: THE EXPONENTIAL GROWTH CURVE   49

Here are some important insights to consider in this time frame:
1. If, at the beginning of 2000, your account value was $100,000, and you contributed nothing more, you didn't break even until 2012. Even though the S&P 500 averaged 3.45% in this time frame (with dividends), you achieved no actual growth because you were earning back what you lost. Arithmetic (average) return vs Geometric (actual) return — that distinction is part of the lost knowledge of Compound Interest that few understand.
2. After the dotcom crash of 2000–2002, you lost around 40% of your money. From 2003 to 2007 your return was 13.11% per year (a total gain of 65.53%), yet you barely recovered from the previous losses. The home runs of 2003–2007 made us forget about the pain of the loss. They convinced us we were winning that whole time, yet we were barely back to break-even. Did you realize that?
3. The home run/strikeout time frame from 2000 to 2007 caused you to lose an entire Compound Cycle.
4. The 2008 crash lost around 37% in a single year. That pain was real. But the home run right after it made all the pain go away. For the next 4 years, you made 14.98% annually, feeling you were winning when 2012 arrived only to make you even, getting you back to your 2000 account value.
5. The homerun/ strikeout time frame of 2000–2012 cost you up to two full Compound Cycles.
6. From 2000 to 2019, the S&P 500 **averaged** 7.67% (arithmetic) with an **actual** (geometric) return of 6.03%. Therefore, you can never trust a financial advisor who quotes investment average. When considering the impact of risk, averages and actuals are not the same value and can be misleading. Always demand ACTUAL returns over 20+ years to determine a reasonable expectation of returns.
7. Some money managers claim to be able to time the market and buy low/sell high to avoid the risk while capitalizing on the loss years, but this is a rare accomplishment and near impossible to do consistently.

One thing I have not touched on is the impact of 3% average inflation (reducing the buying power of your money) or devaluation of the US Dollar. When you add the impact of inflation along with losses, the situation is much worse. Study the inflation-adjusted S&P 500 since 1927, to see the real growth of the stock market. This will blow your mind the same way it blew mine!

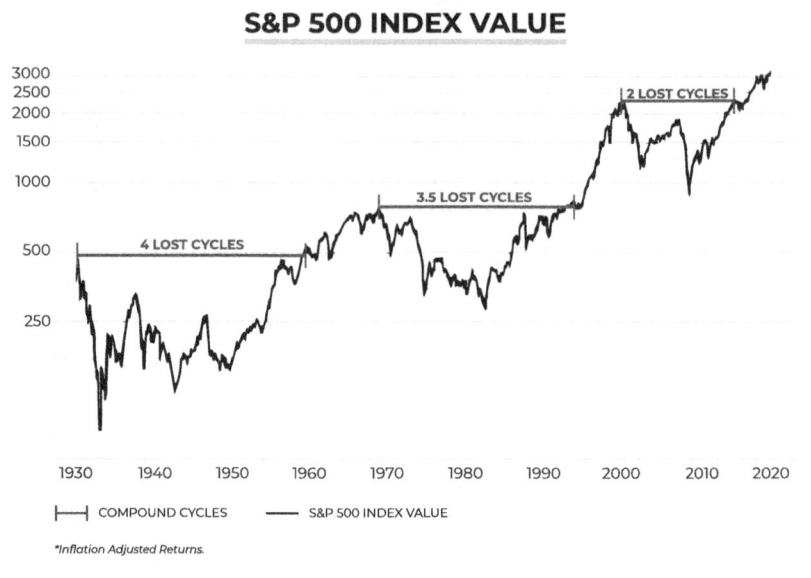

S&P 500 INDEX VALUE

Inflation Adjusted Returns.

This inflation-adjusted S&P Index Value graph shows us just how little compounding occurs inside the Investment Equation. Although S&P 500 Index dividends helped with some additional growth, the results were subpar in producing wealth. At various times over the last 90 years, when loss is present, it takes decades of rebounds to get us back to where we started. It always does rebound, as our financial advisors promises us, but at what cost? We repeatedly miss Compound Cycles.

Even more eye-opening regarding inflation is the recent example of market volatility and market crash caused by the COVID-19 pandemic. In August, 2000, the S&P 500 Index had an inflation-adjusted value of 2,271.97. In March of 2020, the S&P 500 Index was hovering around 2,300. In the blink of an eye 20 years of market growth evaporated due to risk, loss, and inflation. Will it recover? Of course it will! Unfortunately, it may take one month, one year, or numerous years. We just don't know.

And when will the next pandemic, financial crisis, or other volatility arrive again? Impossible to predict!

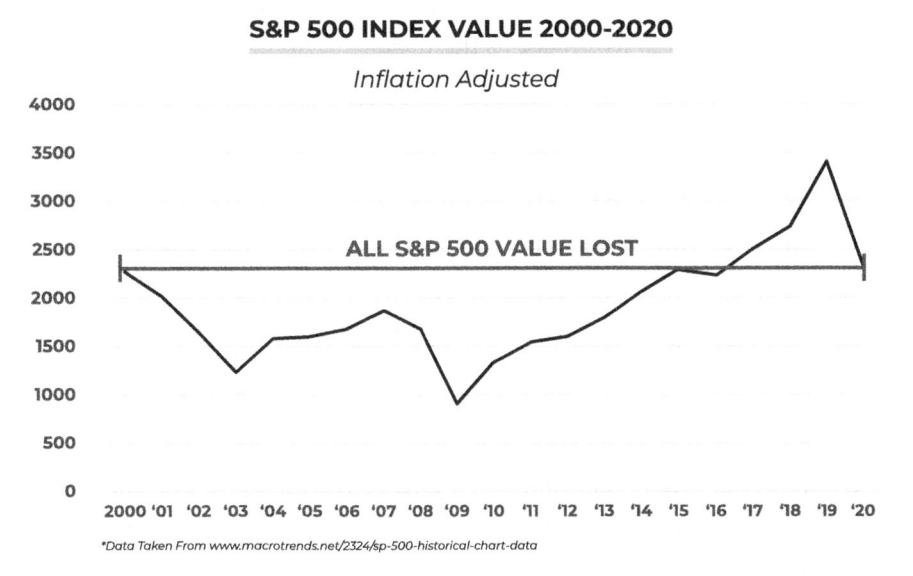

S&P 500 INDEX VALUE 2000-2020
Inflation Adjusted

[Line chart showing S&P 500 index value from 2000 to 2020, with a horizontal line labeled "ALL S&P 500 VALUE LOST" at approximately 2500. Y-axis ranges from 0 to 4000. X-axis shows years 2000-'20.]

*Data Taken From www.macrotrends.net/2324/sp-500-historical-chart-data

Additionally, over the last 90 years, there have been roughly 65 years of plummets, rebounding, and inflation, with only around 25 years of actual growth. As I write this book in March 2020, the S&P 500, with reinvested dividends and inflation adjusted, has produced a growth of only 5.95% since 1930 and 2.49% since 2000. Few pay attention to just how influential risk and inflation really are because the home run behind the collapse makes us believe we are winning. The financial world uses cool terms like "re-balancing a portfolio" or "capitalize on the down market" but the damage has already been done. Lost time!

When considering investment options, I recommend using the most current information on market behavior. Society is evolving so quickly with the influence of the internet, social media, consumer behavior, technology, and accessibility of information, I don't even know if yesterday's market behavior is an accurate predictor.

From 1980 to 1999, the stock market averaged over 19% with an actual return of over 18%. $100,000 in 1980 would have been worth around $1,952,000 by 1999 in the S&P 500 Index Fund. That is incredible—it was near solid home runs with no strikeouts for 20 straight years. This was an anomaly in the stock market during which even treasury bonds earned in excess of 10%. This anomaly has skewed the "market average" numbers that the financial gurus claim as an expectation of returns (even if they cannot legally tell us to expect it, the *average returns* make it into their presentations along with the disclaimer that past performance is not an indication of future results).

Could the market reenact 1980–1999 and again turn the S&P 500 Index Fund into a money-making machine?

Of course it could, and that would be great for everyone. But are you willing to take the chance that great gains with minimal risk is how the market will perform over the next 20–30 years? Ups and downs, risk and reward, volatility and inconsistency—The "Investment Equation" is awesome (+) until it is not (-)!

Investments can be great. They are exciting. They just aren't rational for a long-term financial plan when volatility is part of the equation. Risk and loss are extremely detrimental to your success. Years of volatility can produce zero gains and many missed Compound Cycles, devastating your ability to attain the financial freedom you deserve.

The one concept difficult for people to grasp is that security should be the focus even before considering potential gains. Security first is in direct conflict with the linear mindset of "get rich quick." Security is the cornerstone of wealth and sounds boring, slow, and steady. The linear mind wants the best immediate results at the expense of your long-term success and compounding.

There are tremendous opportunities to make money within the investment equation. The 1990s were a great example of market success. The 2000s were not. The 2010s were great! What do the 2020s have in store?

We have no clue, but history tells us, even with most years being home runs along with a couple of bad strikeouts, it will always lose time in the "rebound." To achieve Exponential Growth, the strikeout (loss) must be eliminated, and that only happens by ignoring the temptations of the potential home run. Any asset based inside of the (+/-) of the Investment Equation will inevitably underperform!

"Learning is the Beginning of Wealth . . . Searching and Learning is where the Miracle Process All Begins"

Jim Rohn

NOTES/ THOUGHTS

CHAPTER 5

The Five Paths of Conventional Financial "Freedom"

Financial gurus and influencers around the world passionately claim there are five strategies to financial freedom. We are told to follow their guidance and that doing so will bring value to our lives, which is partly true. Something is usually better than nothing.

Each of these five strategies draws a different audience based on individual history, concerns, fears, and hopes. After all, anything promoting good money concepts are worthy of our attention. However, there is always a good, better, and best choice available. Which do you want for your life?

In the Wealth Equation of Exponential Growth, $y = a(1 + r)^x$, there are five components as well: **(a)**, **(1)**, **(+)**, **(r)**, and **(x)**. Each component has a simple, elegant purpose in delivering some form of financial freedom.

Let me emphasize that: SOME FORM OF FINANCIAL FREEDOM.

That's why we are all attracted to at least one of the five components. Each one promotes an aspect of the Wealth Equation.

We all have our own biases and gravitate to at least one of the five that resonates with our understanding and beliefs about money.

Wealth is one of the purest forms of energy, so when we have any part of it, it makes us feel good. That may be true, but achieving the fullness of its potential requires all five ingredients.

(a) is the amount of money you put towards your future, which I describe as Pay Yourself First.

(1) represents the critical importance of beginning right now.

(+) reminds us to Protect Our Money from loss, because a loss slows or eliminates compounding.

(r) is our Rate of Return or how fast we can grow our money.

(x) represents Leverage—using external resources (O.P.M—Other People's Money) to accelerate our own growth and effort.

These five components working together produce the best, most sustainable result and is what makes it *exponential*. On their own, each of these components is linear, compelling, feels good, and makes sense to us; we can easily identify each one as a Rule of Wealth.

Influencers make their case with these components individually, building their empires as an expert with a singular focal point. And when that one aspect is important to you, resonates with you, and seems to answer your hopes, concerns, or fears for your future, it becomes your trusted source of wealth knowledge.

I ask you to consider this question: is perspective complete and will it produce the true freedom you are seeking without requiring you to later compromise your dreams with something as destructive as the 4% Rule?

I have personally invested in every example of the strategies/solutions that have been addressed, so far. In each path, an influencer made their case to me convincingly. Diversifying is a common theme of investing that requires you to apply all the components simultaneously to mitigate the risk of any one of them failing. And that is what I did. The results? Not what I expected! Let's go through them one-by-one as they relate to the equation:

$y = a(1 + r)^x$ (YOUR INVESTMENT)

Cash is King!

Those three words are music to the risk averse. What piece of the winning formula is this? PAY YOURSELF FIRST! It is the ultimate source of (a) in the equation. Money flows to you before any other expense. This represents the tangible security of seeing your money in your account (or under your mattress). You have it; you see it, and sometimes you can even touch it.

But what if you stopped at this point?

There is no growth beyond putting in more money, eliminating the power of the (r) and (x) within the rest of the formula. Pay Yourself First isn't enough by itself, especially if you consider the erosion of inflation that brings about an average loss of 3% buying power each year. Every dollar you save is decreasing in value the moment you put it in your bank account or under your mattress.

3% INFLATION LOSS TO SAVINGS

YEAR	PURCHASING POWER VALUE
SAVINGS	$100,000
1	$97,000
2	$94,090
3	$91,267
4	$88,529
5	$85,873
10	$73,742
15	$63,325
20	$54,379
25	$46,697
30	**$40,101**

As you can see, $100,000 cash in an account or under the mattress will have around $40,000 of buying power 30 years from today. When I used to save a lot of money, there were few moments in my life that felt better than holding $100,000 of $100 bills in my hand. This represented the blood, sweat and tears I'd poured into my business. Right in my hand was the tangible proof of my business success! While linear in nature, it felt powerful to have that much liquidity at my immediate disposal. But when I realized that $100,000 had $97,000 of buying power the following year, and $94,090 the year after that, and so on, "Cash is King" was no longer the right answer for wealth and security. It's an incomplete solution!

$$y = a(1 + r)^x \text{ (YOUR COMMITMENT)}$$

Becoming Debt-Free is Freedom!

This strategy is borne of discipline, the sort of discipline required to free oneself from debt as quickly as possible. The call-to-action is always START TODAY represented by **(1)** in the equation. To implement this strategy with priority, live as frugally as possible.

The commitment to this sacrifice comes with its own sense of accomplishment, but at what cost? How much are you Paying Yourself First **(a)**? $0! How much did your money grow **(r)**? $0! How much are you leveraging your money **(x)**? $0!

Once "out of debt," these strategists tell us we can then begin to save using the Wealth Equation. In fact, most of us will always have some debt in our life; therefore, many will use that debt as an obstacle to never begin compounding.

Even worse, the person who focuses entirely on debt takes, on average, 21 years to eliminate it (student loans, mortgages, car loans, etc.). Not to beat a dead horse, but that is three Compound Cycles, potentially worth millions of dollars to your future self.

The singular focus on becoming debt-free leaves you owing nothing and accomplishes nothing beyond the great feeling of being debt-free. This is an accomplishment few ever achieve. What is also true and deeply unfortunate is that it leaves those people ***debt-free*** and ***poor***!

The other day a close family friend, having heard me make the previous argument, came to me and claimed I was all wrong. He had just paid off his house and was proud of the accomplishment. Strong feelings always arise when discussing money issues. I appreciate the discipline of those who tenaciously pay off debt; of course, that feels great. As we continued our conversation about compounding money, becoming debt-free, and various other things, he looked at me and said, "But I sleep well at night knowing I paid off my house." I looked back at him and said, "I get it; that's an amazing accomplishment, but I promise you, you will sleep even better knowing your hard-earned money is making money for you forever!"

Do you know what the bank does with your money when you pay them? Secure it, compound it, and leverage it! Your money paid to *someone else* will never make money for *you* for the rest of your life, but it will make money for them.

Time to repeat myself: You earned the money; therefore, it is yours to make decisions that benefit you FIRST! A decision to pay off your mortgage as quickly as possible rather than applying the Science of Compound Interest could cost you **millions** of dollars in your lifetime. Here is an illustration representing the powerful nature of whether to compound immediately or becoming debt-free first.

3.75% 15 YEAR $300,000 MORTGAGE PAYOFF THEN COMPOUND

YEAR	MORTGAGE BALANCE	MONTHLY MORTGAGE PAYMENT	MONTHLY CONTRIBUTION	ACCOUNT VALUE
5	$219,529	$2,182	$0	$0
10	$120,995			
15	$0			
20	PAID OFF	PAID OFF	$2,182	$177,326
25				$466,695
30				$938,903
40	-	-	-	$2,996,938
TOTALS	-	$392,760	$392,760	$2,966,938

4% 30 YEAR $300,000 MORTGAGE *WITH* COMPOUND FOCUS

YEAR	MORTGAGE BALANCE	MONTHLY MORTGAGE PAYMENT	MONTHLY CONTRIBUTION	ACCOUNT VALUE
5	$236,352			$60,951
10	$219,177			$160,413
15	$193,628	$1,432	$750	$322,721
20	$141,463			$587,584
25	$77,770			$1,019,800
30	$0			$1,725,113
40	-	-	-	$4,754,285
TOTALS	-	$515,520	$270,000	$4,754,285

*Mortgage Payoff in 15 Years vs 30 Years/ *$26,428 Difference Invested in Compounding Immediately. *$9,444 Mortgage Difference Invested in Compounding Immediately. * 4% Mortgage Rate Used to Determine Mortgage Payment. *Assumed Compound Cycles Achieved Every 7 Years.

Paying off debt is very satisfying. Sometimes, we might feel as though we have righted a wrong in our life. I understand why this piece of the Wealth Equation is so satisfying. When "debt-free" gurus and other influencers yell at us to get out of debt, and we do, it feels good. It is very inspiring and emotionally charges our resolve to start immediately. It is a universal Rule of Wealth! Unfortunately, because of lost time in the equation of compounding, you have opted out of having potentially compounded millions of dollars during that same time.

$$y = a(1 + r)^x \text{ (YOUR SECURITY)}$$

Whole Life Insurance (Bank on Yourself), Annuities, and Other Secure Assets!

This appeals to anyone who loves the idea of GUARANTEES! There is a real and emotional sense of safety and security knowing your money is guaranteed by both contract and the financial stability of an A+ rated life insurance company. This feeling is a close cousin to the feeling of CASH IS KING!

It is particularly attractive to many who have experienced market performance extremes: The Great Recession, the Tech Bust, etc. Life insurance focuses on security more than other financial vehicles. By using Whole Life, Annuities, Indexed Universal Life, and some others, they provide contractual guarantees to secure your money. Life Insurance investments are considered some of the most secure assets in the world, on the same level of risk as an FDIC insured bank account.

RISK-RETURN PYRAMID

Risk Pyramid Data Taken From the "KAPLAN CFP Exam Required Education Course 2018."

To receive this guarantee, there are typically some trade-offs. To guarantee the (+) **component of the equation** (the focus on security), the insured receives a lesser rate of return (**r**) and no benefits of positive leverage (**x**).

I often use the phrase "Whole Lifers" to denote those promoting systems called "Bank on Yourself," "Infinite Banking," and other "guaranteed" type systems. Although cash-value life insurance comes with some advantages that are attractive, sound amazing, and have discernible benefit, these systems aren't designed to make much money. Their focus is protecting your money as opposed to compounding it.

This warrants attention when people are being urged to "bank on themselves." The understanding of the trade-off of compounding for the "guarantee" has been lost because the product name, e.g., "Bank on Yourself," sounds so cool. Unfortunately, the math just doesn't support it.

A traditional Whole Life policy has the potential to produce a Compound Cycle in around 14 years; consequently, in 56 years, it will produce around four cycles. A strong compounding account looks to achieve a Compound Cycle in seven years, resulting in eight cycles over the same 56 years. What does that mean to your wealth? Millions of dollars in potential retirement assets and income lost in exchange for guarantees and a cool name.

Here is an illustration of the impact on your wealth using systems like Infinite Banking Concept/ Bank on Yourself, when guarantees are the priority rather than giving compounding the importance it deserves. As an example, how much loss is there with just a $50,000 investment over 56 years? Up to $12,000,000.

COMPOUND CYCLES: 7 YEARS or 14 YEARS

TIME	COMPOUND POTENTIAL	YEARS	COMPOUND POTENTIAL	YEARS
START	$50,000	0	$50,000	0
CYCLE 1	$100,000	7	-	7
CYCLE 2	$200,000	14	$100,000	14
CYCLE 3	$400,000	21	-	21
CYCLE 4	$800,000	28	$200,000	28
CYCLE 5	$1,600,000	35	-	35
CYCLE 6	$3,200,000	42	$400,000	42
CYCLE 7	$6,400,000	49	-	49
CYCLE 8	**$12,800,000**	56	**$800,000**	56

Security and guarantees are not enough to produce wealth! They just don't Compound quickly enough!

$$y = a(1 + r)^x \text{ (YOUR GROWTH)}$$

Home Run Investments!

Traditional investments include those in the form of stocks, mutual funds, index funds, cryptocurrency, and other growth focused investments. Their premise (and loose promise) is to get the best return, usually adding the caveat "over time." It is exciting and enticing to go for the home run of a Bull Market. But at what cost?

Investors forego security! Volatility is the natural consequence when the priority is the rate of return of an investment. The predictable nature of an investment that has the potential for a home run is that it also has the potential to strikeout. This home run/strikeout method of investing provides no warning of its ups and downs, potentially wiping out years of growth and savings in a single afternoon. Mathematically, this requires time (the rebound) to return to where the investor was before the assault, and this loss of time equates to losing one or more precious Compound Cycles.

Most of the population is attracted to this element of wealth. Why are we attracted to this feature even though it brings a tremendous amount of risk and stress to our lives? Because of the simple, flawed concepts of "easy money," "get rich quick," and "no risk, no reward." It is the same psychology that keeps many playing a lottery they will never win because "somebody has to win." We find the home run so attractive that we bypass our survival instincts to protect ourselves. The fantasy of easy money blurs all rational thinking. We cherry-pick a handful of skewed successes promoted heavily on social media, especially those that amplify our internal desire to be rich at all costs, and these expose the money we have to insane amounts of risk.

An example of this paradoxical behavior was the cryptocurrency bonanza of late 2017. In 2-3 months, cryptocurrency went from a word few had even heard to an established phenomenon for which one could find unlimited experts among the average person-on-the-street. To anyone who would listen, these overnight "experts" would promote the inclination to join what was an open Ponzi scheme. Those who had $0 in their account along with an unimaginable debt load, were able to somehow find and invest $1,000-$5,000 in Bitcoin (among various other digital currency) justifying the investment with the fantasy that when this made them rich, they would pay off their debt, be secure, and finally have all the things they wanted.

But they missed an undeniable truth: financial freedom isn't free, it is earned. It is a lifestyle.

The digital marketers used the tagline, "get in now before it is too late," as a technique of emotional manipulation. It sounded intriguing, this new currency, with the growth potential of 10,000x that of real currency. With such a framework, who wouldn't love the possibility of becoming a millionaire, if not a billionaire, almost overnight. In our hearts, we all knew the imagined outcome was impossible, but the desire for "easy money" was so enticing that even the most risk-averse, conservative people I know bought into crypto.

During that brief period in 2017, aunts, uncles, friends, neighbors, and others were contacting me regularly to give me one last chance to make millions on this once-in-a-lifetime opportunity. I didn't bite, because Crypto couldn't provide my money with any security nor any historical data backing its viability. The equation is clear in priority: **(+)** then **(r)**. Security first, then growth is the path to Exponential Growth!

Wealth is an energy source that follows universal laws. It's simple (though not easy) if we can ignore the noise of people looking to manipulate our emotions to earn a buck. Will crypto ever be a viable currency? I don't know, but what I do know is just as George Clason stated in *The Richest Man in Babylon*: *"Gold flees the man who would force it to impossible earnings or who followeth the alluring advice of tricksters and schemers . . ."*

$$y = a(1 + r)^x \text{ (YOUR ACCELERATION)}$$

Leverage!

I find the best example of the use of leverage in real estate investors, business owners, entrepreneurs, and other investments that require a hands-on approach. Because real estate, business, and some other investments are considered hard assets, they have a unique financing option. One can obtain additional funding from lenders by using the hard assets as collateral. This technique is called O.P.M, (Other People's Money), and it is one way to speed up investment potential.

Because leverage has the acceleration potential to spur quick growth and produce significant immediate rewards, it seems a worthy risk to many. While very attractive and exciting, the element of risk lies within many variables encompassed by leverage, including one's individual situation, market conditions, consumer habits, and various other unknowns.

Because the focus of leverage is the (**x**) in the equation, there is no guaranteed security (**+**) and often the value of the hard asset, itself, increases slowly (**r**), typically at the rate of inflation. That is the huge flaw in real estate; its growth follows closely that of inflation (over time), so there isn't really any increase in wealth.

Rather, it simply maintains the buying power of the asset. However, because it is a hands-on approach and leverage is easily accessible, empires can be built quickly using O.P.M. When one asset can secure various assets, such as buying stocks on margin or equity loans in real estate, potential is unlimited.

LEVERAGE

$100,000

$20,000 $20,000 $20,000 $20,000 $20,000

$100,000 $100,000 $100,000 $100,000 $100,000

I believe in (x). I have built my whole career on (x) helping me to rapidly grow my businesses. I believed in my own skill and ability to grow my wealth faster than other investments. This is how most entrepreneurs think. We are wired to believe this. However, as Compound Cycles mature, we soon realize an eternal truth about producing secure, sustainable wealth for the rest of our lives: We may be good, but Compound Interest is better!

John Bogle, founder of Vanguard, is credited with saying, "Never bear too much or too little risk"; in other words, take a balanced view of being neither too risky nor too conservative. To get the results of Exponential Growth, we must balance every ingredient of the formula. All five components play an essential role in this game of wealth. These are what I call the 5 Rules of Wealth!

- **(a)** YOUR INVESTMENT: Somewhere to put money for the benefit of your future self.

- **(1)** YOUR COMMITMENT: Making the decision to begin today.

- **(+)** YOUR SECURITY: Life Insurance provides guaranteed security against loss of your money.

- **(r)** YOUR GROWTH: The Stock Market maximizes the growth potential of your money.

- **(x)** YOUR ACCELERATION: Leveraged O.P.M accelerates your Compound Interest.

All five elements already exist in the market, we simply need to put them together now!

We need one place we can Pay Ourselves First (invest), today (commit), somewhere protected (security), aggressively compounding (growth), and leverageable (acceleration)!

"Every now and then a man's mind is stretched by a new idea or sensation, and never shrinks back to its former dimensions."

Oliver Wendell Holmes Sr.

NOTES/THOUGHTS

CHAPTER 6

The Evolution of Cash Value Life Insurance

The Oxford English Dictionary defines 'evolution' as "the gradual development of something, especially from a simple to a more complex form." I equate that to PROGRESS!

This process is typically subtle, slow, and sometimes barely recognizable until one day, someone notices the dramatic change with the exclamation, "why did no one else ever think of that?"

Because evolution progresses from A to B to C and so on; it cannot go from A directly to Z. Evolution is a sequence of tiny improvements that lead to profound results, similar to the way money compounds.

The landline had to be invented, developed, and improved before creating new technology that led to pagers. Long before the iPhone arrived in 2007, the early pioneers carried the Nokia brick. After the brick came a compact flip phone followed by the technologically advanced Blackberry. Each phase required building upon the success and innovation of the previous phase in order to deliver what had previously been unimaginable.

Evolution is happening all the time in every aspect of society, and each of these aspects evolves at different rates; this holds for financial services, too. The results of these evolutions have a tremendous advantage over the outdated past that they have replaced, especially when the old is subpar. Social media influencer Jay Shetty asserted that seven words have the power to ruin everything: "We have always done it that way!"

Einstein once commented that "great minds have always encountered violent opposition from mediocre minds," a commentary on the way people respond to what seems new and different or challenges conventional wisdom. Most of us prefer the familiar, comfortable with the understanding we've constructed in our minds. Inventors and developers have been ridiculed when presenting concepts and ideas that are not commonplace. One pioneer of the Personal Computer recalls mentioning to his mother what they were creating, and she replied, "What would I do with a computer in my home?"

Index funds, streaming services, smartphones, and millions of other innovative concepts were scorned long before they were embraced. And most cases, these are items some would now claim they could not live without.

Through that same lens, let us examine the evolution of money!

The insurance industry, beginning with Whole life, has evolved, namely, to Indexed Universal Life. These plans have a unique advantage over other investments in the form of security. They provide guaranteed security of your money while also possessing an element of Compound Interest. The compounding effects proceed at a slower rate, because your money is protected from down markets. The result is additional confidence and predictability of your future results, with an eye to retirement income. No other compounding option puts as much focus on security and spendable retirement income as a cash value life insurance plan.

Over time, investing in the Stock Market has evolved; in a world dominated by Index Funds, ETFs and Mutual Funds, the small, non-institutional investor now has access to better tools for online trading and an unparalleled immediacy of information. This created flexibility, balance, and access for all. These instruments have a tremendous advantage over their predecessors because of the slow and steady approach. Index funds were able to reduce costs significantly!

Stock value is subject to the valuation determined by the free market, therefore outside of our control. Consequently, one of the only ways to increase growth is by lowering costs, which remains within our control. Unlike Real estate, the stock market grows for you with little or no effort or follow-up on your part. Investing in an S&P 500 Index Fund is basically investing on autopilot; without making stock or bond choices, your money can grow over time producing an average 8–12% return all by itself. The only requirement is your commitment to invest money and allow it to remain invested as long as possible to achieve as many Compound Cycles as possible. The Stock Market has the most long-term growth potential and is truly "money working for you."

Compared to all other investments, the Real Estate Investment market has evolved rapidly due to its unique advantage: leverage! With interest rates at historic lows, those in the real estate market have mastered the art of leveraging assets to optimize their wealth. Through low interest lines of credit from the bank, a buyer can increase their portfolio size dramatically, while potentially speeding up their rate of return (profit)!

To state the obvious, if buyers had to have 100% of the price of real estate, few would have the means to invest. But persuading a bank to put up 80–100% of the cost of the property, while retaining 100% of the appreciation of its value themselves, is what has created many millionaires in real estate. This is the art of using someone else's money to grow an empire!

Risk lurks in this scheme in the form of market reversals that diminish the value of the asset. In such instances, the borrower may now owe the bank more (in the form of the outstanding principal of their loan) than the property is worth, if it were sold.

In financial services, we have the bad habit of claiming that our singular specialty has the superior advantage, whether it is life insurance, stock market investments, real estate, or something else. But which one offers the most benefit to you and your life? Why do we have to commit to just one?

Here is my radical question: What if we embrace evolution and all the advantages of each perspective simultaneously? What if we could receive the benefits of security, growth, and leverage at the same time and in one place?

That is the definition of Conservative Risk-taking based on the principle of Yin and Yang!—all three amazing benefits (**+, r, x**) combined and optimized into a single platform. Rather than trying to market any individual feature as the be-all and end-all, we have evolved by embracing the entirety of these great ideas. By doing this, we improve and increase the efficiency of the concepts of security, growth, and leverage of our money.

This approach is superior because it builds upon the unique advantages of each component: 1) cash value life insurance protects wealth, 2) the Stock Market grows wealth, and 3) leverage accelerates wealth. These three things are the essence of satisfying the equation:

$$y = a(1 + r)^x$$

The idea that all three principles could coexist was the driving force in the creation of MPI™, an advanced financial strategy focused on efficiency, that brought features and benefits into the mainstream that were not previously available. By using a secure cash value life insurance plan, built with the growth nature and low expense of the S&P 500 Index and amplified using secure leverage, MPI™ provides the path to achieve additional Compound Cycles for anyone!

Remember, just one additional cycle doubles your wealth, so you can imagine the value that multiple additional cycles will provide! The idea and evolution to combine all three is unlike any strategy ever created before.

In 2014, when I first introduced the theory of Compound Cycles as the "true focus" of this evolution, it was not received well. I first brought MPI™ to a financial expert named Eric Palmer, who runs one of the largest financial brokerages in the country. He was recommended to me as being one of the most educated, professional, and ethical people in the industry regarding insurance, stocks, real estate and various other aspects of investing, and financial planning. If there was someone who could understand all three strategies built into one, it would be Eric.

Would you guess how he responded when I explained that these three financial concepts could coexist? "It won't work! It's impossible!"

Luckily for me, although the theory was unique in design, it intrigued Eric. Rather than dismissing the "crazy" notion of evolution applied to investing, he gave me a laundry list of reasons it wouldn't work, but also offered his knowledge and expertise in solving the flaws. If I could find answers to the various holes in the idea, there would be nothing like it.

3 MAJOR MONEY ADVANTAGES

LIFE INSURANCE	STOCK MARKET	REAL ESTATE
PROTECTS MONEY	GROWS MONEY	LEVERAGES MONEY

Throughout the next four years, the fruits of extensive research provided Eric with not only the answers to his questions but also addressed legitimate concerns of lawyers, actuaries, compliance, IRS regulations, and financial advisors. These were all the steps required to release MPI™ to the public; MPI™ gained approval in early 2018.

With this approval, I began to speak publicly to everyone and anyone that would listen. I had designed something that would change the entire landscape of financial planning by increasing security with the predictability of returns while speeding up the compounding effects of money and significantly increasing retirement income.

And MPI™ garnered a second important *approval* in May 2018 from one of the largest A+ rated, mutual insurance companies that had been in business for more than 100 years. Having reviewed, tested, and validated MPI™, they now stood solidly behind providing MPI™ to the public under their brand. MPI™ was no longer just my vision, but an endorsed, backed, and legitimate financial plan offered by one of the world's most fiscally strong, conservative companies.

Naturally, the moment I explained this was only possible through the security of a "cash value life insurance" policy, a large part of the investing population immediately turned away. Insurance has a well-deserved black eye. Even those who listened with interest, typically responded with: "Sounds too good to be true," "That's too easy!," and "No way it works like that!" People had never seen anything like what we had assembled in one solution, so they automatically deemed it "too risky."

And because I claimed that by following MPI™, one could increase retirement income by up to 400% over any cash value life insurance retirement plan, index fund, or real estate rental portfolio, there was skepticism. Given the magnitude of the claim, I understood their responses.

Also, it is the human condition to respond to unfamiliar concepts with skepticism, distrust, fear, and even hate. In the last six years, I have had numerous death threats, received suggestions to kill myself, been described as a Ponzi scheme, called a con artist, labeled a sham, and undergone many other attacks.

But as time went on, actuaries, financial advisors, insurance carriers, lawyers, tax consultants, Certified Financial Planner™ professionals, clients, and many others have analyzed, validated, and ultimately warmed to the idea that the math worked to achieve a better outcome. These individuals have also provided me with additional ideas to improve and maximize Compound Interest inside this MPI™ strategy. Evolution is an ongoing process!

How is it possible that an "evolved" cash value life insurance plan produces these results? Before getting into those specifics, let's review the history of cash value life insurance, its features, its flaws, and the role it plays in achieving Exponential Growth.

There are two main types of life insurance: Term and Permanent. Term, as most people understand life insurance, is a specific amount of death benefit (the amount a beneficiary receives upon the insured passing away) in force for a predetermined amount of time. Most terms range between 15–30 years and provide security to the beneficiaries should the insured die during the term. At the end of the term, assuming the insured is still living, the contract terminates with no remaining value (the money the insured paid in premiums for those 15–30 years is the profit of the insurance company).

The other type of life insurance, which is less common, is called Permanent Life insurance. It typically has a dual function. The first is like term insurance; it provides a death benefit to the insured's beneficiary, but without an expiration date. However, it also functions as a savings account in which any premiums paid above the policy's expenses can grow and compound securely.

"Term" is well understood and often described as *cheaper*. "Permanent" is misunderstood more than it is understood.

TERM VS PERMANENT INSURANCE

TERM INSURANCE	PERMANENT INSURANCE
EXPIRES	PERMANENT, NO EXPIRATION
NO CASH VALUE ACCOUNT	CASH VALUE ACCOUNT
DEATH BENEFIT	DEATH BENEFIT
TAX-FREE BENEFITS	TAX-FREE BENEFITS
LESS EXPENSIVE	MORE EXPENSIVE

The most common type of permanent insurance is Whole Life, and this has existed for a century. Many people also refer to Whole Life in a newer marketing vernacular: *Bank on Yourself* or *Infinite Banking Concept*. Whole

Life policies have some impressive features that are very attractive to anyone who wants to protect their hard-earned money. These features include:

WHOLE LIFE BENEFITS

- LIFE INSURANCE
- LIVING BENEFITS
- TAX ADVANTAGES INSIDE OF 7702(A) TAX CODE
- LEGAL PROTECTIONS
- LIQUIDITY
- LARGE CONTRIBUTION AMOUNTS
- GUARANTEED SECURITY
- COMPOUNDING GROWTH
- TAX-FREE RETIREMENT INCOME
- TAX-FREE WEALTH TRANSFER TO BENEFICIARIES

Various Social Media influencers discuss the benefits of Whole Life as the best wealth transfer system. They even discuss how prominent families like the Rockefellers and others have used a life insurance strategy to transfer enormous amounts of wealth, tax-free, which is all true and great! No other investment platform can produce the tax advantages for wealth transfer like a §7702(a) retirement plan (the IRS code defining life insurance tax benefits).

The benefits sound amazing, right? There is just one problem. It doesn't make much money. It compounds too slowly!

A Whole Life policy provides a non-guaranteed dividend of around 3–6% with a guaranteed floor of around 3–4%. That means no matter what, they will pay at least 3–4% interest on your money. Not a bad thing. Carriers have successfully paid out this annual dividend for a century. This is where the Compound Interest is supposed to be made.

In the 1980s, the average dividend paid over 10%. Deduct your insurance/administration costs from this, and you still could make a near double-digit return inside these plans. Whole Life plans provided guaranteed security and decent growth to the individual, making it very competitive with traditional stocks.

Besides all the benefits listed above, Whole Life became very popular for the high net worth earners, who used it as a tax shelter for estate-planning purposes while enjoying impressive compound growth. As the market inevitably evolved in the late 1990s and into the early 2000s, there were casualties as interest rates declined and Whole Life lost value. It couldn't compete any longer because there were now superior alternatives.

WHOLE LIFE DIVIDEND PAYOUT

YEAR	DIVIDEND PAID
1989	11.50%
1994	9.00%
1999	8.75%
2004	6.60%
2009	7.30%
2014	6.25%
2019	**5.85%**

*Data Came From www.topwholelife.com. *Dividend Payout From the Carrier Guardian Life.

This was a significant moment in the history of Whole Life plans and a pivotal moment in the creation of the IUL (Indexed Universal Life) plan. The once popular Bank on Yourself plan began to lose traction. Rather than producing above 10% returns, it slowed to 8%, then 7%, and now ranges between 3–6% Gross Return. The dividend (less expenses) no longer nets a competitive return compared to a traditional stock investment strategy.

While the plan continues to have many advantages over a stock portfolio, compounding growth isn't one of them. The sales systems of Bank on Yourself and Infinite Banking Concept had come to a fork in the road. They could either dig their heels in and sell solely on the advantages of Life Insurance (tax advantages, security, guarantees, etc.), or evolve by creating ways to grow faster and compete with stocks. The linear motto, "We have always done it that way!" won the day. The wealth transfer tax advantages and a guaranteed (low) dividend became their sales story in which fear was a powerful influence.

The life insurance business, however, has existed more than 100 years for a reason: like any time-tested business, when sales decline, they evolve and adjust. This situation paved the path to the birth of Indexed Universal Life (IUL) in the late 90s (right at the time of the collapse of the high dividend payouts). This new concept provided similar benefits as the original Whole Life contract and could also compete with investment portfolios such as Index Funds in overall returns.

To do this, the insurance company made some trade-offs. Rather than guaranteeing a return of the dividend (3–6%), they would guarantee "no loss," or what we know today as the 0% Floor. Providing a guarantee to never lose rather than a guaranteed minimal win satisfied the Exponential Growth component of security (+). By replacing a rate-of-return guarantee with the 0% Floor, the insurance company could be a little more aggressive with your money to increase the rate of return. Yin and Yang were at play to never lose yet seek to maximize overall returns.

This plan provided a guaranteed return of at least 0% each year (breakeven) with a maximum cap (varies depending on the carrier) commonly credited at the rate of the returns of the S&P 500 Index (without dividends). This floor-ceiling S&P 500 crediting strategy now provided guaranteed "no loss" security and an "actual" aggressive return of around 7–8% (using historical data over the last 30 years) and brought returns similar to the original Whole Life plan during its heyday. Security and growth were now available in one place without the requirement of a guaranteed dividend. Market-level returns without market-level risk and losses. Evolution!

How is it that life insurance can accomplish such a feat? How can they guarantee to never lose, yet still pay around 7–8% on average inside these financial plans?

Back to Yin and Yang and conservative risk-taking. A theory that is so powerful, it seems too good to be true! What I'm about to explain, few people have ever heard, much less considered, which is why, once I provide the details, you will probably respond as most do by saying, "that makes complete sense!"

Of course it does, because it came from a risk-mitigating, unemotional, financially responsible insurance company whose first instinct is to protect, then grow, just as the equation tells us. (+) and then (r).

Within the life insurance company, there is an account called the "General Fund" (see article by *Think Advisor*: "How (and why) Indexed Universal Life Really Works"). This account is where the insurance company's money, including the premiums that policyholders pay, is invested. Typically, the insurance company puts the General Fund in secure long-term AAA bond portfolios, mortgage notes, and various other conservative investments to enable the payment of claims and earn income.

The General Fund is one of the most conservative accounts in the world and has been profitable, year in and year out, irrespective of market performance. Even in extreme down markets (e.g., the Great Recession, dotcom, among others), the General Fund was profitable and paid out a dividend to the Whole Life policy holders. Therefore, it is on the bottom of the Risk Pyramid because it is considered as secure as cash.

RISK-RETURN PYRAMID

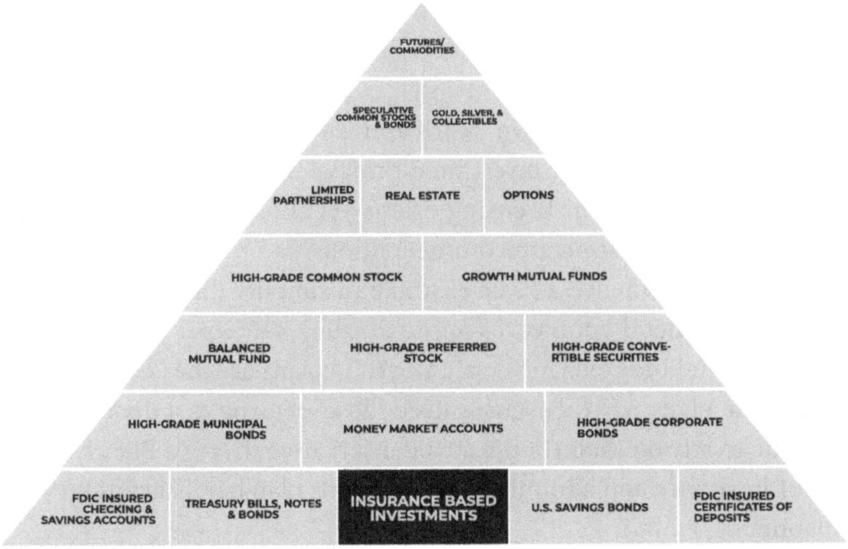
FUTURES/ COMMODITIES
SPECULATIVE COMMON STOCKS & BONDS
GOLD, SILVER, & COLLECTIBLES
LIMITED PARTNERSHIPS
REAL ESTATE
OPTIONS
HIGH-GRADE COMMON STOCK
GROWTH MUTUAL FUNDS
BALANCED MUTUAL FUND
HIGH-GRADE PREFERRED STOCK
HIGH-GRADE CONVE-RTIBLE SECURITIES
HIGH-GRADE MUNICIPAL BONDS
MONEY MARKET ACCOUNTS
HIGH-GRADE CORPORATE BONDS
FDIC INSURED CHECKING & SAVINGS ACCOUNTS
TREASURY BILLS, NOTES & BONDS
INSURANCE BASED INVESTMENTS
U.S. SAVINGS BONDS
FDIC INSURED CERTIFICATES OF DEPOSITS

**Risk Pyramid Data Taken From the "KAPLAN CFP Exam Required Education Course 2018."*

The General Fund account correlates directly with the dividend payout of Whole Life. In the 80s, this account returned more than 10%, because that correlated to what mortgage notes and bonds were paying. It was an anomaly the finance world had never seen before or after the 80s. The insurance company would safely invest the clients' premiums in the General Fund, then use the profits to pay this, once in a lifetime, high insurance dividend.

As time went on and bonds and mortgages produced lower interest returns, the General Fund produced diminishing returns for its clients. When the General Fund began to produce roughly 3–6% (in today's low Bond environment), Whole Life was no longer a viable competitive compounding account. It no longer reflected the balance of Yin-Yang/ Security-Growth, as it had become overweight on the security side and had lost value on the growth side!

For the insurance company to offer the 0% floor and better growth potential, the insurance world brought forth a new idea. In a remarkable example of Yin-Yang balance, one of the most conservative accounts in the world, the General Fund, married with a more aggressive investing concept, the Call Option, (specifically the Bull Spread Call Option Strategy).

This unique General Fund + Call Option strategy is an aggressive form of trading that can accelerate returns when the market is up and eliminate losses when markets are down. Black and white. Options are not an easy strategy to grasp, even for investment professionals; in fact, the majority study them to pass their licensing exams yet choose not to incorporate them into their investment recommendations.

For clarity, I will give a basic example to simplify the math. As mentioned, the General Fund earns approximately 3–6% per year. Both the Whole Life and Indexed Universal Life (IUL) plans use the General Fund. Whole Life plans pay their guaranteed "low" returns as a dividend and continue to rely on their time-tested conservative strategy. But given the cost of insurance and administrative fees, this plan barely keeps up with inflation.

How did the IUL evolve from Whole Life? Because IUL offers credits (interest) that mirror the S&P 500 Index (within the range of the 0% Floor and a ceiling currently between 10% and 15%). This approach increased the average return up into the 7–8% range rather than a 3–6% dividend only.

Here is a diagram that explains what transpires through using the interest earned from the General Fund and purchasing an S&P 500 Index Call Option.

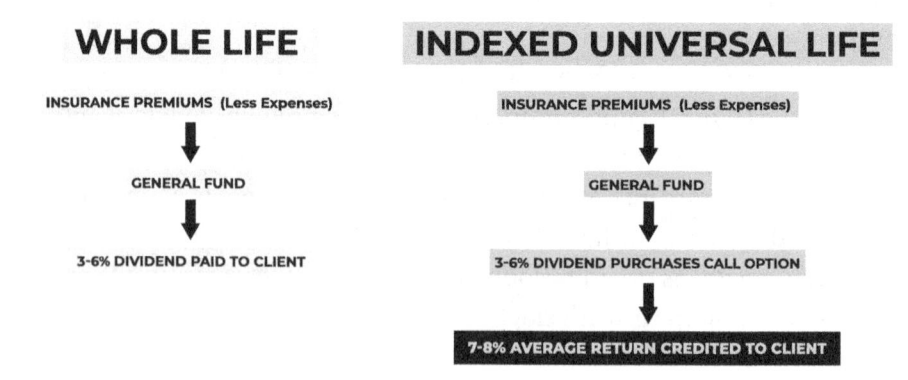

WHOLE LIFE

INSURANCE PREMIUMS (Less Expenses)
↓
GENERAL FUND
↓
3-6% DIVIDEND PAID TO CLIENT

INDEXED UNIVERSAL LIFE

INSURANCE PREMIUMS (Less Expenses)
↓
GENERAL FUND
↓
3-6% DIVIDEND PURCHASES CALL OPTION
↓
7-8% AVERAGE RETURN CREDITED TO CLIENT

The advantage of using the General Fund + Call Option strategy is that your money is never at risk. Your money is always in the General Fund and guaranteed by the insurance company. The most you relinquish is the 3-6% that the Whole Life typically paid in exchange for a 0% floor during down markets.

In a year like 2008, when the S&P 500 was down 37%, rather than making the 3-6% growth of that individual year, you would earn 0%. If you had $100,000 in your account at the beginning of 2008, you would have the same amount at the end of the year (less policy charges). Your principal value had no market risk. This is where the 0% Floor comes from because, literally, your principal value is not at risk in the market.

Looking at the last 90 years of the S&P 500 Index, during 64 years (71%) this Option strategy would have made strong returns for the client. In 26 of those years (29%), the Call Options were worthless (producing 0% returns) "costing" the client the typical 3-6% annual growth of that single year. However, even with that "cost," you break even!

This is the only strategy I have found, after six years of research, that offers a perfect balance of conservative risk-taking. First, eliminating the strikeouts (never lose) and then focusing on maximized growth. Yin and Yang of investing! This strategy has produced net returns of 7-8% over the last 30 years.

Here is an example of how the strategy has performed the last 15 years.

GENERAL FUND PLUS CALL OPTION STRATEGY

YEAR	ANNUAL CONTRIBUTION	PROTECTED CASH VALUE	GENERAL FUND GROWTH	GENERAL FUND RETURNS	CALL OPTION AT RISK MONEY	CALL OPTION RETURNS	ANNUAL POLICY RETURNS	END OF YEAR CASH VALUE
2005		$10,000		$500	$500	$300	3.00%	$10,300
2006		$20,300		$1,015	$1,015	$2,233	11.00%	$22,533
2007		$32,533		$1,627	$1,627	$1,148	3.53%	$33,681
2008		$43,681		$2,184	$2,184	$0	0.00%	$43,681
2009		$53,681		$2,684	$2,684	$5,905	11.00%	$59,586
2010		$69,586		$3,479	$3,479	$7,655	11.00%	$77,241
2011		$87,241		$4,362	$4,362	$0	0.00%	$87,241
2012	$10,000	$97,241	5%	$4,862	$4,862	$10,696	11.00%	$107,937
2013		$117,937		$5,897	$5,897	$12,973	11.00%	$130,910
2014		$140,910		$7,046	$7,046	$15,500	11.00%	$156,411
2015		$166,411		$8,321	$8,321	$0	0.00%	$166,411
2016		$176,411		$8,821	$8,821	$16,830	9.54%	$193,240
2017		$203,240		$10,162	$10,162	$22,356	11.00%	$225,597
2018		$235,597		$11,780	$11,780	$0	0.00%	$235,597
2019		$245,597		$12,280	$12,280	$27,016	11.00%	$272,612

*Contribution Amount After Expenses. *Red Color Denotes Option Producing a 0% Return. *Assuming a 5% Return in the General Fund.

An additional advantage to this strategy is the floor value resets every year on your policy anniversary date after receiving your interest payment for that year. This feature protects not only your principal contributions but also all your gains from previous years. The interest you earn in the good years, is protected by becoming your new principal value, thus assuring that we never step backwards!

"Condemnation Without Investigation is the Highest Form of Ignorance."

Albert Einstein

NOTES/THOUGHTS

CHAPTER 7

Leverage: OPM Made Secure

If there is any flaw to Compound Interest, it is that it is slow and steady, at least in relation to our lifespan. Because it takes time, it cannot produce a scenario of "get rich quick" as that notion is contrary to the laws that govern wealth. In fact, even Warren Buffett has said, "There is nothing wrong with getting rich slowly." You can think of Compound Interest as a way to get rich securely, every time, if you give it the TIME.

Creating a Secure Compound Interest account is like building a Skyscraper. What is needed before you can build up? The Secure Foundation! Packed soil, concrete, rebar, and various other preparations must be in place before you can even consider going up. This is no different with the foundation of Compound Interest. Out before up! When you try to go up before building out, it will fall every single time. Maybe not immediately, but in time; as the weight gets heavier, the lack of a secure foundation will present itself!

Failing to persevere through the first 5–8 years inside of true compounding (the time to accomplish the first Secure Compound Cycle) is why most people fail to reap the benefits of this unlimited power. They quit too soon because the linear mind convinces them they can bypass risk and become rich faster. Remember, "…he who understands it, earns it." We are indoctrinated to believe in emotions of being fast and exciting, to make the most money now at all costs. We want to see results immediately. Unfortunately, that is contrary to the Science of Compounding and an impossibility within the cornerstone of security.

SECURE FOUNDATION

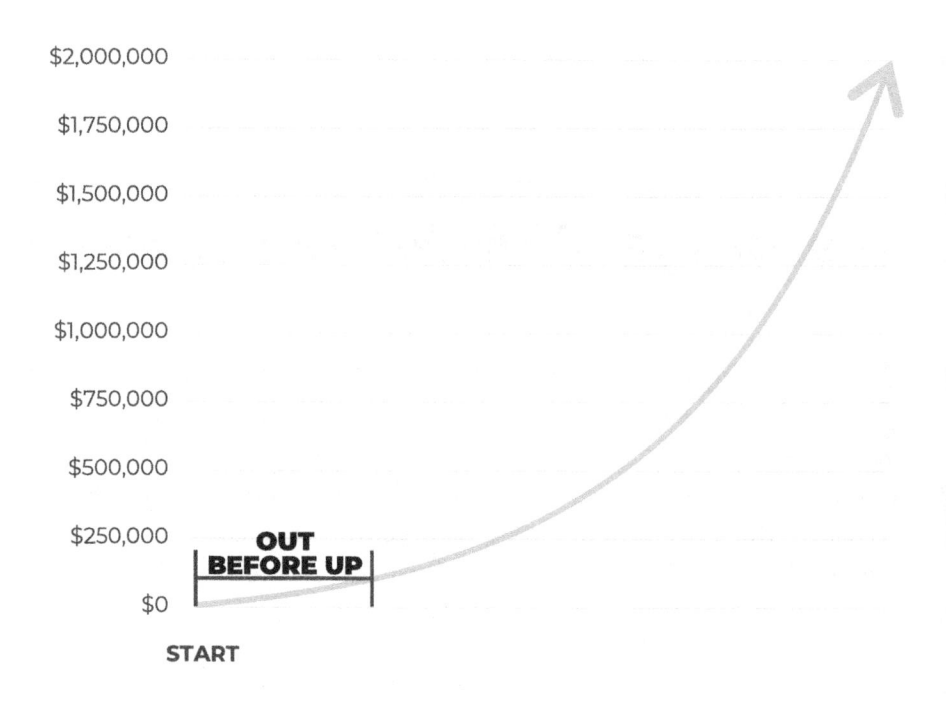

```
$2,000,000

$1,750,000

$1,500,000

$1,250,000

$1,000,000

 $750,000

 $500,000

 $250,000      OUT
              BEFORE UP
      $0
            START
```

As you can see in this compounding illustration, the growth is minimal in the first Compound Cycle. Once you achieve the first Compound Cycle going out, you have built a foundation to begin to go up, and as time goes on, the rate of "up" accelerates faster and faster. You merely had to build the secure foundation first, and then give it time to work its magic.

Traditional insecure compounding attempts to accomplish this in reverse. The goal is to go up as quickly as possible, regardless of what foundation is built, and that is why it consistently falls down. We are taught to chase the rate of return, which we are biologically inclined to do. The #1 question I am asked when in conversation about MPI™ is "what is the rate of return?" I always have to remind the individual that this is the wrong question and what should be asked is "what is my rate of security inside my rate of return?" The difference in those two questions can be one of the most influential understandings regarding your money.

Chasing rate of return early in the investment, while putting yourself at risk, is one of the many reasons we fail to achieve True Compound Interest and the future we dream of! Just look how little affect the first five years really have with a secure rate of return or an aggressive risky rate of return (which is not sustainable)!

SECURE VS RISK-BASED FOUNDATION

YEAR START	INVESTMENT ANNUAL	7% SECURE GROWTH TOTAL COMPOUND VALUE	12% RISK-BASED GROWTH TOTAL COMPOUND VALUE
1	$10,000	$10,700	$11,200
2	$10,000	$22,149	$23,744
3	$10,000	$34,399	$37,793
4	$10,000	$47,507	$53,528
5	$10,000	$61,532	$71,158

$9,619 DIFFERENCE

For "potentially" only an extra $9,600 over 5 years, you were willing to put your money at extreme risk. I understand we all want the best rate of return, but focusing on the long-term within Secure Compounding is the key to maximum benefit. The first 5–10 years, whether building a foundation or going for home runs, produces minimal difference, so building a long-term plan not only has superior long-term results, but very similar short-term results also.

I often get asked, "How can one accelerate their Compound Interest benefits if it takes time to mature?"

There really is only one way. To achieve all the benefits of True Compound Interest, it depends upon the frequency and quantity of Compound Cycles. This is attained based on the amount of investment and the time given to mature. Here is an example of how money + consistent returns + time = amazing results and how increasing investment upfront + the same time provides results that are even more amazing. You want the best results,; get as much money compounding as soon as possible!

$5,000 ANNUAL INVESTMENT

YEAR	INVESTMENT	RATE OF RETURN	ACCOUNT VALUE
1			$5,400
5			$31,680
10			$78,227
15	$5,000	8%	$146,621
20			$247,115
25			$394,772
30			$611,729
	TOTAL INVESTMENT $150,000		**TOTAL INTEREST EARNED** $461,729

$150,000 ONE-TIME INVESTMENT

YEAR	INVESTMENT	RATE OF RETURN	ACCOUNT VALUE
1	$150,000		$162,000
5	-		$220,399
10	-		$323,839
15	-	8%	$475,825
20	-		$699,144
25	-		$1,027,271
30	-		$1,509,399
	TOTAL INVESTMENT $150,000		**TOTAL INTEREST EARNED** $1,359,399

As you can see from the chart, money and time contribute significantly to the outcome. How did an investment of $150,000 produce 3x more interest than $5,000 invested incrementally over 30 years? In the first chart, you'll notice that at year 15, the $5,000 has compounded to around $150,000. The second chart has you investing the entire $150,000 at once. In doing so, you bypassed the 15 years of time required to reach $150,000 in the first chart. This enables your Compound Cycles to begin at a much larger amount. Investing more in the beginning is the most profitable choice you can make to speed up the time required to produce wealth through compounding.

One thing about Compound Interest that even the most sophisticated mathematicians fail to realize is every investment you make has its own Compound Schedule. So money you invest today, will produce its own Compound Cycles, doubling according to its growth, making it the most valuable and powerful investment in your life. Investments you make in year 2, will be the 2nd most powerful and influential in your pursuit of wealth and freedom. Here is an example of a $5000 contribution and the potential growth as time goes on. Giving more time to the same amount illustrates the true power of Compounding! Many people tell me they feel they are "too late" to take advantage of Compound Interest; however, through assets you already possess, including a home you own, equity in a rental, savings accounts, inheritance, retirement accounts, and various other sources, it is never too late for anyone to increase the security and compounding of their money.

POWER OF COMPOUNDING WITH TIME

$5,000 ONE TIME INVESTMENT POTENTIAL

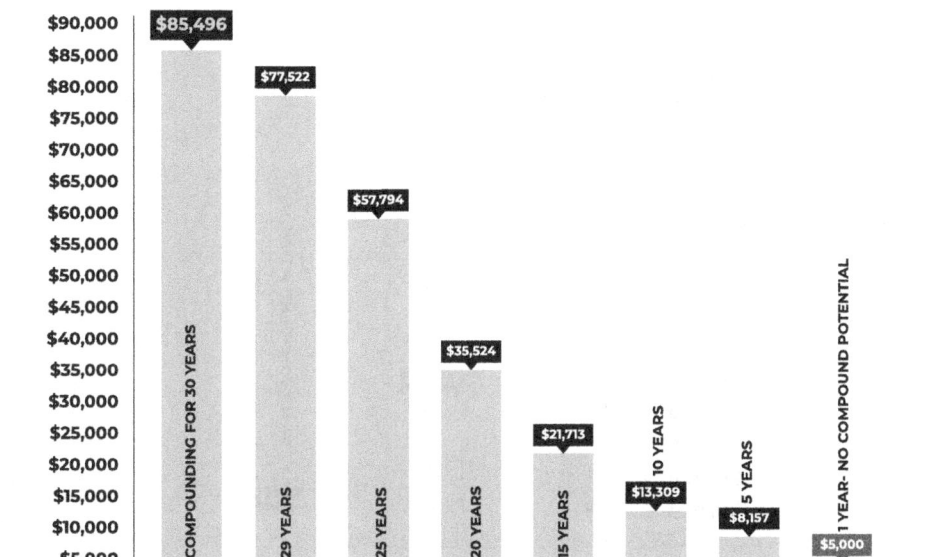

30 YEARS	$85,496
29 YEARS	$77,522
25 YEARS	$57,794
20 YEARS	$35,524
15 YEARS	$21,713
10 YEARS	$13,309
5 YEARS	$8,157
1 YEAR - NO COMPOUND POTENTIAL	$5,000

*Assuming a 7 Year Compound Cycle.

Why this is so important to realize is because every dollar you can invest as soon as possible into a Secure Compound Account, will provide you with your absolute best future. For example, if you were to invest $5,000 today or wait one year, the delay would lose your money $7,974 of Compound Potential. Every year you delay your money loses significant Compound Power!

What happens to your potential if you invested $10,000 in the first year rather than $5,000? Your potential would double, increasing the compounding of your money over 30 years to $170,992.

You would achieve an extra $85,496 by investing $5,000 more in the first year. But what if you invested the $10,000 on the 15th year rather than the 1st year? Or waiting till the 30th year? What loss would you experience when eliminating time from the equation?

POWER OF COMPOUNDING WITH TIME

$10,000 ONE TIME INVESTMENT POTENTIAL

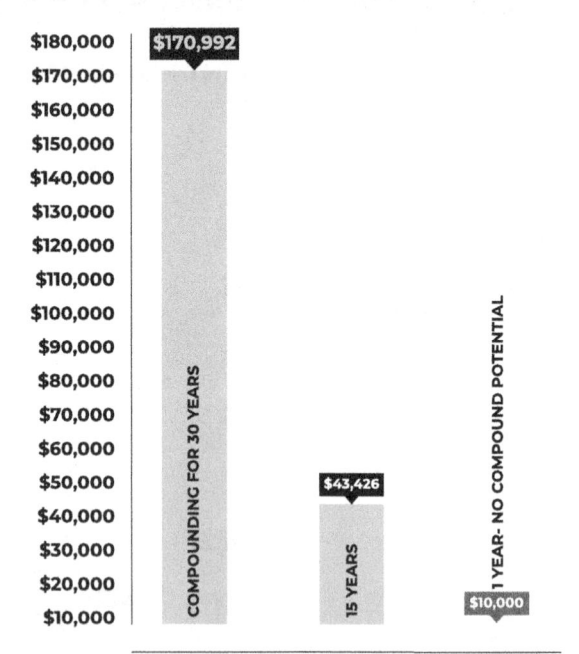

Compounding for 30 Years	15 Years	1 Year - No Compound Potential
$170,992	$43,426	$10,000

*Assuming a 7 Year Compound Cycle.

$127,566 of lost Compound Interest waiting 15 years to begin or $160,992 waiting 30 years.

In order to maximize Compound Interest in your life, investing as soon as possible, as much as possible, is the most reliable way to achieve the future you want and deserve. Waiting to start investing after you get out of debt, or buy a house or car, or any other perceived priority in your life could cost tens or hundreds of thousands, if not millions of dollars to your future self. The best outcome comes from secure investing immediately because losing time has more lost potential than even the risk inside of the investment equation.

Many people tell me they feel they are "too late" to take advantage of Compound Interest; however, through assets you already possess, including a home you own, equity in a rental, savings accounts, inheritance, retirement accounts, and various other sources, it is never too late for anyone to increase the security and compounding of their money. Putting money into a Compound Cycle Schedule today rather than waiting even one year from now, will provide anyone the best Compound opportunity.

Success is always about optimizing the next Compound Cycle with choices we can make today. When we look at the mainstream investment strategies, a common rule is used to determine how often a cycle (doubling of money) occurs. The calculation is called the Rule of 72. Simply divide 72 by your net interest earned; the result is the duration of a Compound Cycle.

MAINSTREAM RATE OF COMPOUNDING

ACCOUNT TYPE	RATE OF RETURN	TIME PER COMPOUND CYCLE
CASH	0%	NEVER
SAVINGS ACCOUNT	0.01%	720 YEARS
SINGLE FAMILY EQUITY	4%	18 YEARS
WHOLE LIFE	5%	14 YEARS
LOW COST S&P 500 INDEX FUND	6%	12 YEARS
INDEXED UNIVERSAL LIFE	7%	10 YEARS

*Returns Taken From 2000-2019. *Returns Average Net of Fees. *IUL Returns Vary Depending on Carrier Caps.

If you had $100,000 invested in each of these letting it compound since 1999, what is the result? Furthermore, what would it look like in another 20 years at the same growth rate?

$100,000 INVESTMENT FROM 2000-2039

ACCOUNT TYPE	RATE OF RETURN	ACCOUNT VALUE 2000	ACCOUNT VALUE 2019	ACCOUNT VALUE 2039
CASH	0%	$100,000	$100,000	$100,000
SAVINGS ACCOUNT	0.01%	$100,000	$100,201	$100,401
SINGLE FAMILY EQUITY	4%	$100,000	$219,000	$480,000
WHOLE LIFE	5%	$100,000	$265,000	$703,000
LOW COST S&P 500 INDEX FUND	6%	$100,000	$320,000	$1,028,000
INDEXED UNIVERSAL LIFE	7%	$100,000	$386,000	$1,493,000

*Returns Average Net of Fees. *Estimated Returns Taken From 2000-2019 and Same Returns Repeated for 2020-2039.

If Compound Cycles are the solution to reaching our most prosperous future, how can we safely speed up the rate of cycles? By itself, your money has limited potential to achieve full financial freedom, as all current investment methods don't compound quickly enough. The growth of traditional investments, including real estate, index funds, and the new and improved IUL, still takes 40 to 50 years before it produces the necessary Compound Cycles to achieve the wealth most desire. Therefore, to shorten the time, we need a supercharge. This supercharge is called leverage, also known as O.P.M. (Other People's Money)!

This one financial concept can make you more money than anything else because of what it can do for you: accelerate Compound Cycles! By cutting even a few years from a cycle, your lifetime wealth can increase by 2x (1 additional cycle), 4x (2 cycles), 8x (3 cycles), even 16x (4 additional cycles).

Conversely, when used in a risky manner, there is no other strategy that can devastate wealth faster than leverage. Why? Because leverage can compound losses and destroy multiple Compound Cycles in the blink of an eye. Rather than bypassing time with a lump sum, it can have the reverse effect. Consider the 2008 Great Recession, the first down market the economy experienced when substantial leverage was easily accessible to the masses!

Financial Leverage is the process of borrowing money, typically from a bank, and investing that money somewhere that earns more than the borrowing costs. If you borrow money at 4%, you need at least 5% earnings for leverage to work profitably! This process is the Holy Grail of all investments because you can double, triple, or even quadruple the amount of money working for you! Although the leveraged money is not yours to keep, it provides you with many buckets of money, each creating Compound Interest. You keep all the gains the leveraged money produces. If the market is going up, and you are making more than what the money costs to borrow, you have sped up how much money you are making. This process compounds your money at a very rapid pace, cutting years from a cycle. Anyone who is a risk-taker and wants to maximize the use of their money loves leverage!

However, this process is also tremendously risky. If there is any downturn in the market that reduces the value of your investment, the whole process collapses in the blink of an eye. Everyone imagines they can time a downturn and get out early enough to avoid the risk, but 2008 shows this is nearly impossible to do because, as investors, we want just one more win, one more deal, and then we will get out. It's a Gambler's Mindset. "Feels Good!" But then Armageddon hits fast and hard in the form of stock or real estate downturns, business struggles, or various other events that can cause leverage to implode! Not only did asset values drop around 40% in 2008, the borrowed money you invested also dropped 40% in value, yet you still owed the full loan, and you were still required to pay the interest on that loan. This quadruple whammy set the world on fire. Most leveraged investors lost everything in 2008 when they could not sell their *asset* for at least as much as the outstanding loan.

But what if there were a way to leverage, to supercharge your investment, without the traditional risk of down markets that implode your investments? This is the concept of Secure Leverage using Yin and Yang: prioritizing security first, eliminating as much risk as possible, and then maximizing every opportunity, resource, and feature available to speed up your Compound Cycles.

This is what I mean by **SECURE LEVERAGE**. You've likely never heard these two words together, because until now, they have never coexisted.

Secure Leverage is the science (and art) of using O.P.M. without the traditional risk. Given this safe access to accelerate your wealth, how often would you leverage if that were possible? Typically, I hear, "All the Time!" But there are also skeptics saying, "Impossible!" Welcome to the evolution of O.P.M.!—Secure Leverage made available to everyone to create a process to safely accelerate compounding regardless of income level, debt level, gender, education, credit score, or any other *condition* that most leverage strategies require, making them accessible only to the wealthy or well-connected.

From the beginning, against the advice of counsel, I have been completely transparent regarding the inner workings of what I've been describing in this book, on podcasts, in conversations, etc. Many wise people have suggested that I limit how much I say to keep it proprietary, protected, and even hidden as it could be bad for business to unveil the "secret sauce." But I feel this knowledge and education should be available to everyone, not just those I happen to encounter, as this is a huge component in *The Lost Science of Compound Interest!*

Secure Compound Interest is a Universal energy, and everyone should have access to it because the world will be better off. Everyone deserves this knowledge, whether they employ my services or not. And frankly, I take pride in the education I provide above anything else. Critics lose fuel in the light of facts and transparency while investors gain financial freedom in that same light. Everyone wins! So here comes the magic.

The Yin and Yang of investing, as explained, is the theory that both security and growth must coexist to achieve the best long-term result. Within a single platform, a **correctly designed** Indexed Universal Life or IUL (explained in more detail later, as the design is vitally important) has both guaranteed security (in the General Fund) and compounding potential (in the Call Option strategy).

Let me pause here to acknowledge that there are flaws in any plan, this one included; however, many of the comments I've seen online reek of misinformation, lack factual reference, and often reflect the opinion of an uneducated financial advisor who fears competition. Math doesn't lie. Follow the math! This includes taking the formula for Exponential Growth and asking your own trusted advisor(s) to create a strategy for you following the Wealth Equation.

Let's keep going. Most life insurance companies have an amazing feature inside their IUL plans called a Participating Loan, a loan using the cash value in your policy as collateral. It is called "participating" because even after using it as collateral, it remains in the General Fund + Call Option strategy earning interest. This loan was variable in the past in that the insurance company could charge any interest rate with few restrictions. This made using the Participating Loan from the insurance company risky and unpredictable because if they charged more interest than your account was producing, negative compounding (decay) would occur.

Then, in 2017, a unique loan feature was presented by most of the insurance companies: A Participating "Capped" Loan. This loan offered clients a maximum (cap) rate the insurance company could charge, ranging between 4–6%, guaranteed for life. This loan has no arbitrary limits in size, no underwriting, credit checks, commissions, or origination fees because it's a dollar-for-dollar collateralized loan against the cash value in your MPI™ plan. No matter what the amount of money you have in your cash value, you can take a loan of similar size from the insurance company.

The Participating Loan is also a permanent loan, meaning no repayment is required because your cash value always secures the debt and this will be paid back at your passing. It is not as complicated as it might sound. It is a simple lifelong dollar-for-dollar collateralized loan, and this eliminates the risk for the insurance company to your benefit. This is one feature necessary to achieve the security and wealth you desire.

PARTICIPATING CAPPED LOAN

- **COLLATERALIZED AGAINST CASH VALUE**
- **GUARANTEED LOAN RATE CEILING FOR LIFE**
- **NO REPAYMENT TERM**
- **NO CREDIT CHECK**
- **NO UNDERWRITING**
- **NO COMMISSIONS**

How is getting a loan from an insurance company different from other types of loans? It is the key to Secure Leverage, the link that will provide a path to wealth for anyone who wants to understand and embrace it. After I explain this key, you will think to yourself, "That sounds too easy." But money was always supposed to be easy. We complicated it by striving for home runs built on speculation. As you begin to embrace singles and doubles in the form of slow, steady, and secure, thus allowing money to compound for you and do all the heavy lifting, you will come to realize that wealth is simple if you can bypass the linear infatuation of "get rich quick." Further, this is a win-win strategy. Your financial well-being and that of the insurance company are both made better with no one having to lose!

Inside of insurance retirement plans, there is a word that gets thrown out often: Arbitrage!

Although this word is often used incorrectly, in the insurance world, it is important to understand the context. In layman's terms, Arbitrage, when used in reference to the Participating Loan, is interest earned vs interest paid! If you can make more on the loaned money than what it costs to borrow it, you earn an arbitrage spread. Inside of an IUL that achieves an average return of around 7–8%, with the availability to borrow money costing 4–6%, something amazing occurs that I've yet to find in any other investment/retirement vehicle: Internal Arbitrage. Borrowed money making money for you. Increased Compound Interest. Accelerated Compound Cycles. All done by itself securely!

Here is how we do it:

Let's say you have $10,000 in Cash Value (CV) in your MPI™ account. This $10,000 is earning you historically around 7–8% (I'll use 7% for easy math). By using this CV as collateral to the insurance company, they will give you a loan of nearly $10,000. You can use this money for whatever you want. You can use the money for a new car, to pay off debt, start a business, or take a vacation, it is your choice. The insurance company is protected because your money is still in your account with a lien on it to support the loan, but you have an additional $10,000 to use how you see fit. Your money is still earning around 7%, their money is costing you around 4%, so even after you spend the $10,000, you are still earning on average around 3% net.

This sets an IUL apart from Bank on Yourself or any other leverage system I am aware of. It internally earns arbitrage even on the money you are spending. Mathematically, your money should continue to grow for you indefinitely at an average rate higher than what it is costing you.

But all this scenario did was slow down your Compound Cycles from 10 years to 24 years (Rule of 72). With this scenario, taking a loan from the insurance company doesn't seem like a good idea to because it slows down your growth from 7% to 3% on average, simply to spend money on a vacation, a car, payoff debt, start a risky business, or whatever else you choose to do with your money. Instead of using the loan for such linear matters, we have a unique opportunity to maximize the compounding.

Put Yin and Yang into effect with that extra $10,000 from the Insurance Company. Protect it and Grow it by doing the same thing we did with our original money. We take the $10,000 and put it back into the General Fund and the Call Option Strategy! When we do this, the borrowed money is 100% protected by the 0% Floor, and we now have an additional 4–6% interest earned from the General Fund to increase the amount going into the Options to produce this additional 7% average. Add this new 7% to our original 3% (7% – 4% loan) and we just compounded the compound.

After this process of Secure Leverage occurs, we now have $20,000 in the account, $10,000 has a lien on it (protecting the insurance company's loan), earning around 3% interest. The loan amount is new money to do as we see fit, and because we want to protect it and grow it, we put it right back into the system that earns 7% on average. We are now making around 10% interest on "our money." More importantly, we have increased the speed of Compound Cycles from every 10 years to every 7 years on average.

Here is an illustration of the process:

CASH VALUE COMPOUND INTEREST

CASH VALUE	RATE OF RETURN	LOAN RATE	INTEREST EARNED
$10,000	7%	0%	$700

LEVERAGED COMPOUND INTEREST

LEVERAGED VALUE	RATE OF RETURN	LOAN RATE	INTEREST EARNED
$10,000	7%	4%	$300

MPI™ COMPOUND INTEREST

CASH VALUE	LEVERAGED VALUE	RATE OF RETURN	INTEREST EARNED
$10,000	$10,000	10%	$1,000

*10% Rate of Return Calculated From $1,000 Interest Earned / $10,000 Cash Value. *Calculations for Illustration Purposes only and Not Assumed as a Guarantee.

Because your Cash Value (CV) before the loan was $10,000, and then dropped to $0 after they put a lien on it to collateralize the loan, and then went back to $10,000 when you deposited the new money to your account, you now have your liquidity and cash value back. There is no liability to you like a traditional loan. Of the $20,000, $10,000 is collateral for the loan so the insurance company is satisfied and protected, and $10,000 is liquid, so your money is your money.

Guess what we can do again? The same process, compounding the compound yet again, speeding up the Compound Interest through leveraging of the insurance company's money, and converting it to Secure Leverage by following the General Fund + Call Option strategy.

This use of leverage executed efficiently inside of the MPI™ system increases Compound Cycles, setting most anyone up for full financial freedom. As the MPI™ system matures, just as Compound Interest is supposed to do, it increases its speed. We start at around 7% growth, and by adding additional 3% buckets (less expenses) spilling into our Cash Value bucket rather than increasing the individual rate of return and incurring more risk, our collective internal rate of return goes from 7%, to 8%, to 9%, to 10%, to 11%, and so on as time marches on.

We need not focus on increasing individual rate of return by putting ourselves at risk, but on achieving secure returns optimized with Secure Leverage. The MPI™ system is stable with around 7% secure returns on average, therefore, we don't need the home run if we never strike out. Instead we are accelerating opportunities available through Secure Leverage. Evolution!

Even saving $250 a month, used in the Secure Leverage system, can produce millions of dollars in the lifetime of an individual who begins immediately and commits. It's simple! It was never about the rate of return but the rate of compounding.

Maximum compounding is not about timing the market, trying to buy low and sell high, but about the amount of time you can compound. Timing the market has little to no value in the MPI™ Secure Leverage system and why building you Secure Foundation immediately has more value than "when" you buy in. Security does protect your money, which is good, but more importantly, protects your time. You cannot get time back once it is lost.

Achieving wealth doesn't take a super skill set, or the secret stock, or ground level investment. In MPI™, the money is used conservatively, market risk is eliminated, and many leverage buckets repeatedly pour into your main bucket resulting in the magic—the acceleration of Compound Cycles!

Advisors and clients alike often say "why has no one ever done this before?" Key aspects were not available until 2017. Evolution is the collection of progress over time, from Einstein explaining Compound Interest, to the advent of Whole Life insurance using the General Fund, to John Bogle developing the low-cost Index Fund, to Indexed Universal Life with the hybrid account (General Fund + Call Option strategy), and finally, to the Participating Loan at a contractually capped rate for leveraged money.

Sound too good to be true? There must be risk involved to achieve accelerated returns, right?

The answer is of course; nothing is risk-less. However, at this point you're likely wondering, how risky is this system and what happens in a down market when you leverage through the General Fund + Call Option strategy? Because this is important to know, there will be math – a LOT of math – in this explanation!

If you would like any additional explanation, please reach out to me and I will be happy to clarify any question in full transparency and accountability. I intend this detailed explanation to build confidence in the fact that wealth, security, and freedom are available to anyone who wants it! I also maintain a YouTube Channel with various videos explaining a lot of these concepts.

www.YouTube.com/c/CurtisRay

CURTIS RAY
ALWAYS BE COMPOUNDING!

@iamcurtisray @iamcurtisray @iamcurtisray

CHAPTER 7   LEVERAGE: OPM MADE SECURE   101

To begin, let's imagine that after 10 years of using Secure Leverage, you now have $300,000 in your secure account, comprising a Cash Value (liquidity) balance of $100,000 and a Participating Loan balance (leverage) of $200,000 (a 2 to 1 leverage ratio). As mentioned, all the money is making a return of 7% on average, but we are paying around 4% interest on the leverage account, therefore we net (earn) 3% on the leveraged balance.

But what happens when a year like 2008 hits and the S&P 500 is down nearly 40% in value? Are we devastated, seeing a big chunk of our hard-earned nest egg wiped out? NO! Time to show you the power of Secure Leverage!

SECURE LEVERAGE

CASH VALUE (LIQUIDITY)	+	PARTICIPATING LOAN VALUE (LEVERAGE)	=	SECURE ACCOUNT VALUE
$100,000		$200,000		$300,000

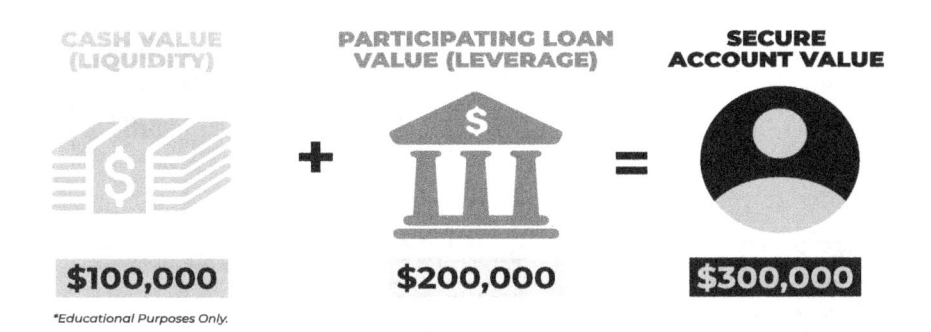

Educational Purposes Only.

I will use conservative assumptions of a 0% Floor and an 11% Cap in an IUL, although there are many IULs with higher Caps than 11%.

As mentioned, $100,000 of Cash Value, which is liquid in our account, earns the full interest credit amount ranging from 0 to 11%. Another $200,000 in Leverage will also earn the same range of 0 to 11%; however, we will pay 4% interest on it no matter what the market returns. Therefore, the NET return on the leveraged money has a floor of −4% and a ceiling of 7% (the 4% cost is deducted from the original floor and ceiling). Various carrier loans have caps ranging from 4 to 6%.

Let's apply some math with an example in a down market:

You have $300,000 in your secure account, $100,000 Cash Value, $200,000 Leveraged Value. At the end of the year, the market blows up.

What happens to your account?

The $300,000 is protected by the 0% Floor regardless of how far down the market may drop. Because you had $200,000 leveraged at 4%, there is an $8,000 interest payment due ($200,000 x 4%). Rather than paying $8,000 out of pocket, this $8,000 can be added to the *leveraged* side of the ledger!

Your $100,000 CV, or what is liquid, will convert to $92,000 because, rather than paying $8,000 in interest, the insurance company will put an additional lien of $8,000 against the CV. $8,000 of your money will be part of leverage rather than CV, which will make your Leveraged Value $208,000.

SECURE LEVERAGE AFTER 2008 MARKET CRASH

NEW CASH VALUE (LIQUIDITY)	+	NEW PARTICIPATING LOAN VALUE (LEVERAGE)	=	NEW SECURE ACCOUNT VALUE
$92,000		**$208,000**		**$300,000**
$100,000 (PREVIOUS CASH VALUE)		$200,000 (PREVIOUS LEVERAGED VALUE)		
- $8,000 (4% PARTICIPATING LOAN RATE OF $200,000)		+ $8,000 (4% PARTICIPATING LOAN RATE OF $200,000)		

*Values Do Not Include Policy Expenses and Are For Example Purposes Only. * Assumed 4% Loan Rate. *Loan Rates May Vary By Carrier

Did you notice that $92,000 + $208,000 still equals $300,000?

The 0% Floor protected the full account value, eliminating the traditional risk of leverage. What did happen was the ledger, or ratio of liquidity to leverage, adjusted according to the down market, but the value in your account earning interest remained unchanged. This mechanism would allow us to take years and years of consecutive down markets before being exposed to any catastrophic risk.

No other leverage system operates this way, always focused on protecting the total amount of money in your account to earn full interest when the market is performing and fully protect the account value when the market turns downward.

It is vital to success that we avoid, at all costs, taking a step backward, losing Compound Cycles. Then, when the market rebounds, rather than rebuilding losses, we pick up where we left off ($300,000). Let's continue the example so I can show you the powerful nature of what I'm illustrating here.

In the following year of our hypothetical 2009, the S&P 500 soars to a return of 27%, giving us the full 11% interest credit (the ceiling), with the following result:

$300,000 is the starting full secure account value, comprising $92,000 of Cash Value receiving 11% or $10,120. $208,000 of Leveraged Value would receive 11% or $22,880. That's a total interest gain of $33,000 (11% of all $300,000). Then, we must pay interest of $8,320 (4% of $208,000). All said and done, we have made a NET gain of $24,680, in other words, a return of roughly 27% on policy Cash Value ($24,680/$92,000). Through a secure plan with a maximum earning cap of 11% but "securely leveraged," we can earn similar to the "home run" years of the S&P 500 Index Fund **without** the downside risk of the market.

Let's update the ledger:

Total Secure Account Value: $324,680 (starting balance of $300,000 + $24,680 net interest)

Cash Value: $116,680 (starting value $92,000 + $24,680 of net interest earned that year)

Leveraged Value: $208,000.

SECURE LEVERAGE AFTER 2009 MARKET REBOUND

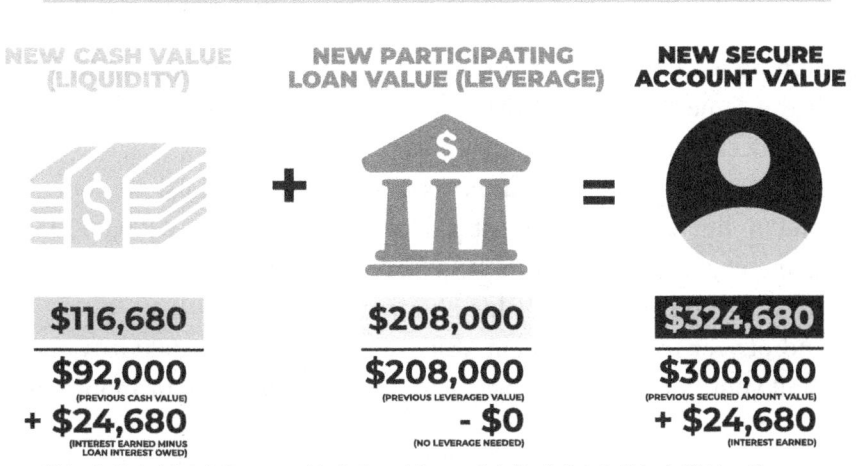

NEW CASH VALUE (LIQUIDITY)	NEW PARTICIPATING LOAN VALUE (LEVERAGE)	NEW SECURE ACCOUNT VALUE
$116,680	$208,000	$324,680
$92,000 (PREVIOUS CASH VALUE)	$208,000 (PREVIOUS LEVERAGED VALUE)	$300,000 (PREVIOUS SECURED AMOUNT VALUE)
+ $24,680 (INTEREST EARNED MINUS LOAN INTEREST OWED)	- $0 (NO LEVERAGE NEEDED)	+ $24,680 (INTEREST EARNED)

*Values Do Not Include Policy Expenses and Are For Example Purposes Only. *Results Projected Using An 11% Interest Cap. Assumed 4% Loan Rate. *Loan Rates May Vary By Carrier.

In 2008, while others in the S&P 500 index lost nearly 40%, our *cost* amounted to a journal entry to pay interest on a future date (4% of journaled interest versus a 40% decline in value). During the rebound, we had an increase in both our total account and cash value. Leverage ratios vary over time, sometimes reaching 5 to 1, but produce similar results every time there is a down market and then a rebound. In our back tests, we typically had more CV (liquid money) in our account after the rebound than before the correction.

Can this be accomplished in any other traditional leverage system? Let's do the math!

TRADITIONAL LEVERAGE

CASH VALUE (LIQUIDITY)	+	LINE OF CREDIT VALUE (LEVERAGE)	=	INVESTMENT VALUE
$100,000		$200,000		$300,000

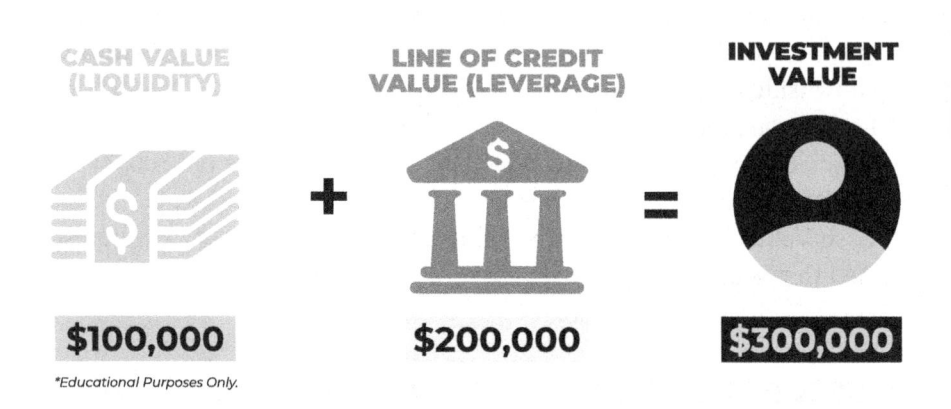

Educational Purposes Only.

Beginning with $300,000 in a traditional leveraged investment in 2008 with the same scenario, $100,000 of your money, $200,000 leveraged. Market declines by 37%, what happens?

The $100,000 Cash Value plummets to $63,000. A 37% loss. Additionally, an $8,000 line of credit interest payment is due on the $200,000 loan reducing our Cash Value from $63,000 to $55,000.

The $200,000 Leveraged Value plummets to $126,000.

End of year total Investment Value: $181,000. A $119,000 loss, more than all your liquidity in the account. You lost 100% of your money and incurred debt.

TRADITIONAL LEVERAGE AFTER 2008 MARKET CRASH

NEW CASH VALUE (LIQUIDITY)	NEW LINE OF CREDIT VALUE (LEVERAGE)	NEW INVESTMENT VALUE
$55,000	**$126,000**	**$181,000**
$100,000 (PREVIOUS CASH VALUE)	$200,000 (PREVIOUS LEVERAGED VALUE)	$300,000 (PREVIOUS INVESTMENT VALUE)
- $37,000 (37% LOSS DUE TO MARKET RISK)	- $74,000 (37% LOSS DUE TO MARKET RISK)	- $119,000 (LOSS DUE TO MARKET RISK AND LINE OF CREDIT LOAN INTEREST)
- $8,000 (LINE OF CREDIT LOAN INTEREST OWED)		

*Values Do Not Include Policy Expenses and Are For Example Purposes Only. *Results Projected Using the S&P 500 Index Returns with Dividends. *Assumed 4% Line of Credit Loan Rate. *Loan Rates May Vary.

In 2009, the big rebound year, the market went up 27%. What is the end-of-year Cash Value?

$55,000 of Cash Value earning 27% = $69,850 minus the $8,000 loan payment due for 2009 or $61,850.

$126,000 of leveraged money earning 27% = $160,020.

TOTAL INVESTMENT VALUE AT THE END OF 2009: $221,870.

TRADITIONAL LEVERAGE AFTER 2009 MARKET REBOUND

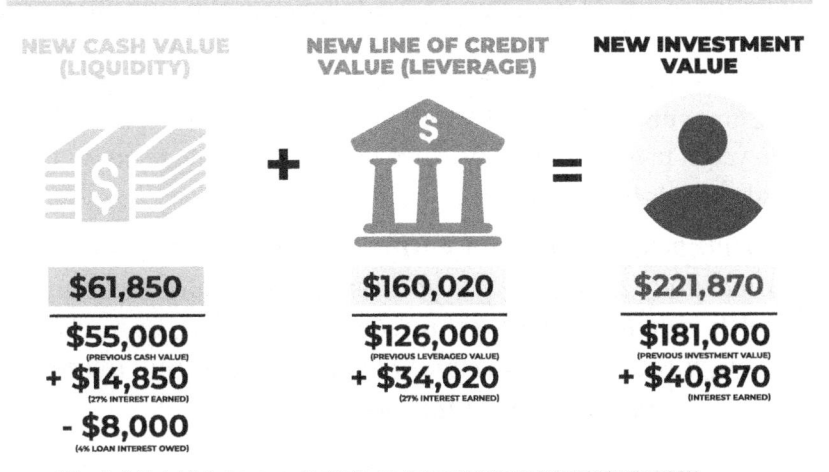

NEW CASH VALUE (LIQUIDITY)	NEW LINE OF CREDIT VALUE (LEVERAGE)	NEW INVESTMENT VALUE
$61,850	**$160,020**	**$221,870**
$55,000 (PREVIOUS CASH VALUE)	$126,000 (PREVIOUS LEVERAGED VALUE)	$181,000 (PREVIOUS INVESTMENT VALUE)
+ $14,850 (27% INTEREST EARNED)	+ $34,020 (27% INTEREST EARNED)	+ $40,870 (INTEREST EARNED)
- $8,000 (4% LOAN INTEREST OWED)		

*Values Do Not Include Policy Expenses and Are For Example Purposes Only. *Results Projected Using The S&P 500 Index Returns with Dividends. *Assumed 4% Line of Credit Loan Rate. *Loan Rates May Vary.

Consider: $324,000 total value after the crash and rebound in Secure Leverage. $221,000 total value in the traditional crash and rebound scenario using leverage, each having started with $300,000.

Magnify leverage with multiple down years in a row like the three years of the dotcom bubble/bust. Secure Leverage would still be strong. The 0% Floor would have protected our account value by adjusting the cash value to the leverage side of the ledger until the rebound occurred. What happens to traditional stocks or real estate in consecutive years of down-markets using leverage? Complete and utter devastation that few can survive, much less recover.

Secure Leverage was built on risk mitigation and to provide security against the unknown. It is not 100% risk-free. A straight decade of consecutive market decline could break this system. In an apples-to-apples comparison, when other investments fail in multiple-year down markets, MPI™ remains strong! Leverage enhances all returns, but Secure Leverage does it with confidence, allowing us to weather a storm in which we'd otherwise fail!

My familiarity with the process of Secure Leverage was borne from the six years of research and evolution spent designing and developing. Few can speak to the same level of detail that you hear from me simply because I had to create it from scratch. I have run thousands of simulations to stress various assumptions: to determine exactly when to begin leverage, how much, how often, and how to minimize the risk of multiple down years, as well as other layers of security to assure the best possible outcome.

The evolution of Secure Leverage paved the way for MPI™ (Maximum Premium Indexing). MPI™ is the process designed to optimize this Secure Leverage opportunity and eliminate as many unknowns and risks as possible. It is a sequence of choices that when followed, speed up the rate of Compound Cycles from every ten years, on average, to every six to seven years, making wealth available to anyone willing to go get it. He who understands it, earns it!

> *"Attempting to succeed without embracing the tools immediately available for your success is no less absurd than trying to row a boat by drawing only your hands through the water or trying to unscrew a screw using nothing more than your fingernail."*
>
> **Richie Norton**

NOTES/THOUGHTS

CHAPTER 8

The Pure Compounder

Though I've shared a lot of information with you, what's coming next will blow your mind. The true potential of your money and the power of Compound Interest in your life is like nothing you have considered in the past. Now, it is time to explain the knowledge that was truly "lost" regarding Compound Interest in today's world of finance.

In 1926, George Clason wrote a book called, "The Richest Man in Babylon," which sold millions of copies. If you haven't read it yet, consider it *strongly recommended* by me and my team. Many have heard of this book, considering it was first published in 1926, and most of those who have read it believe it to be an outstanding story on the simplicity of money. It is so much more than that. Inside this book lies a secret about money that is so powerful it can literally change the course of your life.

I have referenced a phrase dozens of times in this book, and it is a common saying in the finance world today, but what does it truly mean and why do I call it "The First Rule of Money"?

What is this rule? **Pay Yourself First!** This seemingly simple concept suggests that you work hard, but always keep the first portion of your money for yourself, and with a modest compounding of your money, a tremendous benefit accrues. This investment in your future is first, ahead of all other expenditures of any type. There are no exceptions to this rule. None. You work hard to earn money and you deserve to reap the reward first, before anyone else, and that means before paying down debt, rent, mortgage, food, recreation, gas, cell phone, etc. You first, then the rest! Get the order wrong, and you'll kill compounding potential, and you'll never see the benefits it can bring for you and those you care about. Because we have been conditioned to believe our liabilities come before our future needs, most people never achieve the power of Compound Interest in their life!

Pay Yourself First is the First Rule of Money because it is the only way to benefit from the power of Compound Interest. This is money working for you for the rest of your life, growing ever higher by following the Exponential Growth formula, $y = a(1 + r)^x$. *Pay Yourself First* is the First Rule of Money, the (a) in the equation is the key that unlocks the full potential of your money by creating the seed that will grow to unlimited benefit through the amazing theory I call "The ABC of Wealth!" Always Be Compounding!

Always Be Compounding! Think about how simple that is: focus your efforts on compounding your life. You accomplish this by first taking baby steps, a little here, a little there, while always trying to avoid any steps backward. If you always focus on compounding your money, you will achieve not only financial stability in your life, but financial abundance every single time. This fundamental rule applies to many areas of life: If you always focus on compounding your marriage, you will have a fulfilled, ever-progressing relationship. Health? The results are always the same when you commit to always compounding!

I want to inspire you to open your eyes to the possibility of "Always Be Compounding" in your financial life with every dollar you ever make. This will become an evolving process as you mature in your understanding and commitment to Compound Interest. Imagine where you'll be if all your hard-earned money went to your future self, compounding and speeding up the rate of cycles. Consider your future if all your money you made continued to make money for you forever? Your money is like a full-time employee who hires other employees, whose role is to improve your life, working 24/7 for free, with no holidays, vacations, sick days, or needs beyond your commitment to protect them.

Are you willing to protect your money from dying? It originates with Pay Yourself First! Your money is your money to keep! One thing most people fail to understand is that paying other people before paying yourself is allowing your money to die. When you give your money to someone else, does that money have any potential of creating future wealth for you? Of course not. You have given the compound potential to the person receiving your money. It is now dead to you.

Conversely, if you could keep every dollar you ever earn and it continued to work for you, every single dollar compounding for your future, then you've truly built an unbreakable foundation! This is the true "Science of Compounding" made available to anyone and everyone. It is possible, and I will explain the pinnacle of compounding right now.

Let's review two scenarios, calling them the Traditional Compounder and the Pure Compounder. We learn "Pay Yourself First" by putting at least 10% of income towards our future. The Traditional Compounder, named Erin, does exactly that. Erin makes $50,000 a year, fully believes in Compound Interest, pays herself first with $5,000 (before anything else) and lives on a $45,000 budget. Erin is doing exactly what she should to reach her dream of financial freedom. She invests $5,000 annually, compounding at around 7% interest ($350 of interest earned the first year) that will grow to around $450,000 in 30 years, producing a mediocre annual retirement income of around $18,000 (The 4% Rule). If she saved $10,000 a year, the results would double. She did everything right, but still ended up with a low retirement income.

What happened to the $45,000 of earned income she spent on her budget? Was it used at its full potential? No, because 90% of her work died the moment she spent it, never to earn any interest. 90% of her efforts provided compounding energy to someone else.

Good, better, and best! Throughout this book, I have used the terms "cause and effect" and "sequence of events" in various parts. It is now time to bring it all together and explain what a Pure Compounder is, the peak of money efficiency, someone who lets none of their hard-earned money die, earning Compound Interest from every dollar they ever earn for the rest of their life.

To accomplish this requires literally and mathematically every single component in the $y = a(1 + r)^x$.

(a) – Pay Yourself First
(1) – Today
(+) – Somewhere Secure
(r) – Somewhere Compounding
(x) – Somewhere Liquid and Leverageable

The Pure Compounder understands a special philosophy of money stated as "the wealthy never use their own money for anything." What does that mean? It means the wealthy know how much power and potential their money has, so they are always compounding their money. When they need money to spend for expenses, they leverage it from someone else at a lower cost than their compounding potential.

To illustrate using the same example as above, Erin one day reads this book and discovers the "Science of Compound Interest" for herself and is determined to become a Pure Compounder. It takes determination to evolve from a Traditional to a Pure Compounder; it doesn't happen overnight. Once Erin achieved this status, rather than paying herself $5,000 a year to compound and use $45,000 for her expenses, she begins paying herself $50,000. Every single dollar she makes goes to herself, as it is her money to keep. She earned it. She is now making around 7% interest on all $50,000, or around $3,500 annually. However, she still has a living expense of $45,000.

This is where O.P.M. (Other People's Money) done right comes into the equation. It is the **(x)** factor! Liquidity and Leveragability! Having the opportunity to securely leverage money (0% Floor inside the General Fund plus Participating Loan Feature) at around 4%, she can take a line of credit against her own cash value, all $45,000 needed for living expenses, costing her $1,800 in interest owed ($45,000*4%= $1,800). $3,500 earned minus $1,800 owed = $1,700 of net earned interest on average rather than $350 from the Traditional Compounder! A $1350 increase in Compound Interest because she understood the simple laws that govern Pure Compounding.

And after this transformation, what does her account and retirement income look like? Around $900,000 and a retirement income of $108,000 a year! In this example, the same amount of money was being spent on life—therefore, no difference in lifestyle—but through the Science of Compound Interest, she let none of her hard work go to waste, her money never died. This is the power of the ABC of Wealth!

CHAPTER 8   THE PURE COMPOUNDER

TRADITIONAL COMPOUNDER	
INVESTMENT	$5,000
RATE OF RETURN	7%
INTEREST EARNED	$350
COST OF LIVING	$45,000
INTEREST EARNED	$0
TOTAL INTEREST EARNED	**$350**

PURE COMPOUNDER	
INVESTMENT	$5,000
RATE OF RETURN	7%
INTEREST EARNED	$350
COST OF LIVING	$45,000
INTEREST EARNED	**$1,350**
TOTAL INTEREST EARNED	**$1,700**

*$45,000 Budget Paid Through the O.P.M. Feature With an Assumed Loan Rate of 4%. *Loan Rate May Vary.

Your money is your money to keep and compound! Use someone else's money for all expenses as much as possible, assuring it is secure and collateralized.

How can this be possible? A scenario where 100% of your money is compounding for you for the rest of your life? It's simple . . . follow the Wealth Equation. If you are willing to Pay Yourself First, immediately placing it somewhere that offers extreme security, but also provides aggressive growth, as well as liquidity and leveragability, pure compounding is achievable.

The score is "interest earned vs interest paid." That is the big flaw with Bank on Yourself/Infinite Banking; interest earned (after expenses) is typically less than interest paid, causing a decline in wealth every time it is leveraged. But if you can produce a positive spread, your compounding effects are sped up and optimized.

What I have demonstrated is a get-rich-SLOW program; becoming a Pure Compounder does not happen overnight. It usually takes the Traditional Compounder 5–8 years to mature into a Pure Compounder; therefore, it is essential to begin immediately. Some attain the goal sooner, depending on their situation, but success is about evolving toward and embracing the power of compounding in your life as soon as possible. It takes time. Everything of worth takes energy, discipline, and security to achieve. "Eliminate Risk; Maximize Reward" is the true path of prosperity!

I want to provide a few examples of how this works to spark your imagination of the power your money has to work on your behalf. The decisions you make now will completely transform your future self and the freedom you have at your disposal.

FUN MONEY

Many of us save around $5,000 a year (maybe more or less, but the principle remains the same) earmarked for vacation/fun money. We work hard for this money, hoping to have a great experience, make some memories, bond with our family and friends, and renew ourselves.

What happens to your money once you spend it? Gone! Dead! It has become someone else's compounding potential now.

By living the ABC of Wealth (Always Be Compounding), you commit to the best for your future self. Rather than save and spend, you compound, then spend! (**x**) pays for everything. Cause and effect! That $5,000 has the potential to earn you conservatively 7% growth on average per year. Because we have liquidity in the account, as you need money for your recreation or vacation, you can leverage (borrow) it at a rate of around 4%, earning a net 3% interest on average, even after you spend it on a vacation.

You read that right; you can make money even on the money you spend! You would spend it anyway; you might as well make money off it! Do you know what that 3% interest on $5,000 will make for you in your lifetime (assuming you are 35 and living to 85)? An additional $17,000. That may not sound like much, but when you do this every year, it adds up to hundreds of thousands of extra dollars, if not millions, of wealth in your life. This is just one example of a regular expense in a cycle of earn, save, and spend. Consider the power of compounding when using this strategy for your mortgage/rent, utilities, food, and various other items and you will soon realize that compounding is the most powerful force in your life.

PAY OFF DEBT

Many of us earn, save, and pay down debt. This is a great benefit to your life. On a path to becoming debt-free, you save interest you otherwise would have paid. You might be convinced to put a larger down payment on a house to lower your mortgage payments. But in doing so, you also opted out of becoming a Pure Compounder.

I am not against paying off debt; it is a good thing. What I am against is using money inefficiently by making decisions that don't produce the best outcome. In the flow of becoming a Pure Compounder, the requirements are, first, an understanding that your money is yours to keep; second, the criticality of qualifying your money in a compounding system; and third, using the growth of your money as a source to pay off debt, a down payment for a house, or the means to achieve any other financial goals you may have. The order in which we use our money is what creates the potential of becoming a Pure Compounder.

There are many more examples I could provide to show the benefit of prioritizing compounding ahead of everything else, but the result is the same: It follows the Exponential Growth equation of $y = a(1 + r)^x$. When you follow the order correctly, it's perfect. It never fails. It will produce unlimited wealth for you and use your money as efficiently as possible.

You must be asking, why has no one ever done this before? Why is this not taught to everyone? Because it takes all five components working in harmony, which, until 2017, was not a secure option because all five components were not available until then.

I explained some of this in previous chapters, but I reiterate: To achieve this compounding phenomenon, required a mechanism enabling us pay ourselves today—somewhere it would be extremely secure, achieve sufficient growth (need not be a home run), and would be liquid and leverageable. All three factors are essential. We need the cake and the ability to eat it.

From six years of research, I discovered only one platform available in the financial world that could provide all the ingredients necessary to become a Pure Compounder. We just need to put it together now! And that is what I did—I put all the pieces together!

TRADITIONAL COMPOUNDER

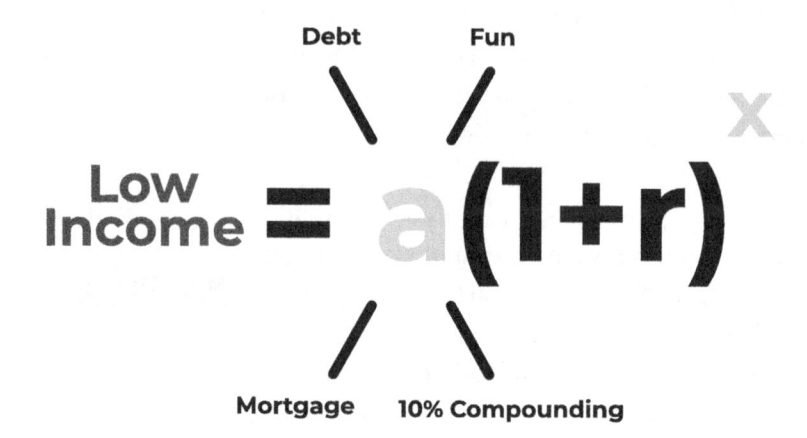

$$\text{Low Income} = a(1+r)^x$$

- Debt
- Fun
- Mortgage
- 10% Compounding

PURE COMPOUNDER

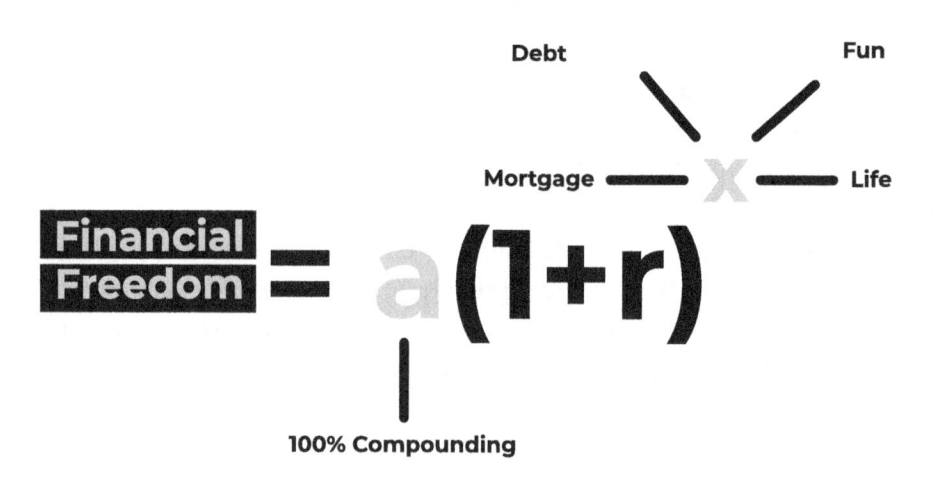

$$\text{Financial Freedom} = a(1+r)^x$$

- Debt
- Fun
- Mortgage
- Life
- 100% Compounding

"Money is Plentiful for Those Who Understand the Simple Laws Which Govern Its Acquisition."

George Clason

NOTES/THOUGHTS

CHAPTER 9

MPI™: Good to Great

I urge you to pause a moment and do something you might not be accustomed to. I encourage you to speak with other financial service professionals if what I have explained so far is not bringing you hope and excitement for your future. Why? All planning is good planning when done for your benefit, even if other plans don't encompass all five components of $y = a(1 + r)^x$. Not everyone *fits* with my philosophy and vice versa. To embrace my extreme focus on compounding before anything else is not something everyone can wrap their head around.

I advise you to begin Paying Yourself First and compounding immediately, even if you don't yet believe or understand what I have disclosed so far. Building those two good habits in your life will only bring value to you. However, for those who see the value in the scientific and mathematical power of the Exponential Growth equation and have the desire to become a Pure Compounder, start your path immediately.

One size may not fit all . . . But ALL SIZES FIT ONE: Compound Interest! No matter who you are, where you come from, or what your situation is, protecting, compounding, and securely leveraging your money is for everyone!

As mentioned, among positive choices, the possibilities are good, better, and best; which one do you choose?

The financial world clings to one key mantra: **DIVERSIFY**, spread investments among solutions that are a mix of good, better, and best.

Diversification: a method of money management whereby an investor reduces the volatility (and thus risk) of his or her portfolio by holding a variety of different investments that have low correlation with one another.

What does that mean in effect? Mitigate your risk with a variety of investments, because the chances of them all collapsing simultaneously are highly unlikely; however, almost everything will lose eventually! Think about how backwards that is. Rather than focusing on eliminating risk from the entire portfolio, the traditional financial industry's primary advice is to avoid the collapse of all your assets at the same time. Put some here, put some there, hope for the best, but assume that at least one category will lose money from time to time. "But don't worry, it will rebound!"

A children's song called *"The Wise Man Built His House Upon a Rock"* illustrates this principle perfectly. Consider the lyrics:

> The wise man built his house upon a rock . . .
> The wise man built his house upon a rock . . .
> The wise man built his house upon a rock,
> And the rains came tumbling down!
>
> The rains came down and the floods came up,
> The rains came down and the floods came up,
> The rains came down and the floods came up,
> And the house on the rock stood firm!
>
> The foolish man built his house upon the sand,
> The foolish man built his house upon the sand,
> The foolish man built his house upon the sand,
> And the rains came tumbling down.
>
> The rains came down and the floods came up,
> The rains came down and the floods came up,
> The rains came down and the floods came up,
> And the house on the sand fell down!

This song, although very simple, has a valuable lesson we can learn. Build upon a rock! Build slow, steady, and secure. Building upon sand is quicker, easier, and it rarely rains (I'm from Arizona, so rain is literally a rare occurrence). But *rare* is not the same as *never*. Everything is fine and dandy until it is not. The sandy foundation cannot work over a long period of time to achieve the best results. Because it *WILL* rain.

MPI™, Maximum Premium Indexing, is an entirely new way of thinking about wealth creation. The notion that you can build a single platform focused on security first, the rock, such as a General Fund within a life insurance company that has been profitable for more than 100+ consecutive years, and then push every limit possible without ever foregoing the foundation of security. Results begin slowly, then, as compounding takes root, they accelerate through maturity, satisfying all the demands of Yin and Yang: Protect, Grow, and Leverage!

MPI™, soon to be a household name, is a financial strategy created in 2014 with the preconception that modern diversification was flawed from the beginning, being more destructive than constructive—in essence, it is multiple houses, all built on a foundation of sand. It merely segmented risk into separate spaces rather than eliminating it.

Though improbable that you would lose all your houses simultaneously, such a situation is a constant risk that requires a rebound each time it rains, and then, after we lick our wounds, where do we rebuild our house?

Until 2014, the only choice was to rebuild upon the same foundations of sand where our house had been destroyed. Time to quote Einstein (again), *"Insanity is doing the same thing over and over again and expecting different results."* He could have easily called that his theory of linear thinking.

The financial industry uses a theory called the *Risk Pyramid* to explain the levels of risk inherent in various investments. The goal of this theory is to continually place investments that appear lower on the Pyramid without compromising too much growth potential. When you invest lower on the Pyramid without losing any growth potential or even increasing your growth potential, you have achieved the optimal goal in investing. Less risk, same or more reward. If you go up the Risk Pyramid for less or same return, diversification has a reverse effect; it becomes inefficient and tremendously lowers the probability of your long-term success.

RISK-RETURN PYRAMID

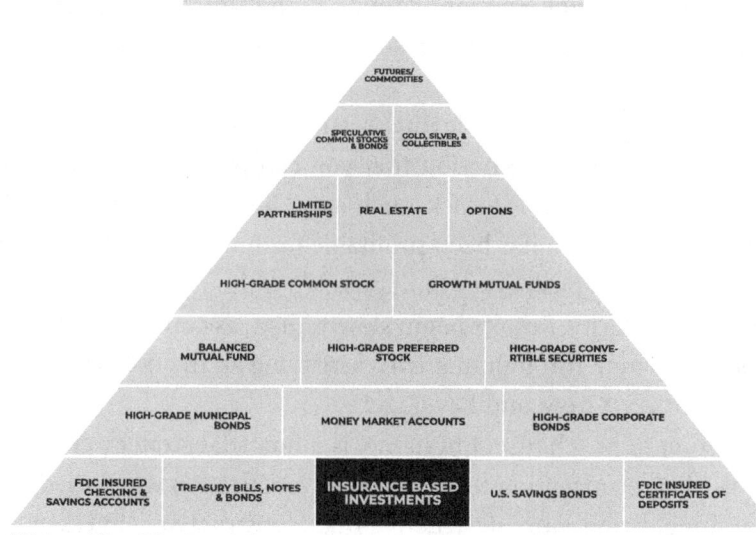

```
                        FUTURES/
                       COMMODITIES
                  SPECULATIVE
                  COMMON STOCKS    GOLD, SILVER, &
                     & BONDS       COLLECTIBLES
              LIMITED
           PARTNERSHIPS    REAL ESTATE      OPTIONS
         HIGH-GRADE COMMON STOCK      GROWTH MUTUAL FUNDS
          BALANCED      HIGH-GRADE PREFERRED   HIGH-GRADE CONVE-
        MUTUAL FUND          STOCK            RTIBLE SECURITIES
     HIGH-GRADE MUNICIPAL                          HIGH-GRADE CORPORATE
          BONDS         MONEY MARKET ACCOUNTS           BONDS
      FDIC INSURED                                                FDIC INSURED
       CHECKING &    TREASURY BILLS, NOTES   INSURANCE BASED    CERTIFICATES OF
    SAVINGS ACCOUNTS       & BONDS             INVESTMENTS      U.S. SAVINGS BONDS   DEPOSITS
```

*Risk Pyramid Data Taken From the "KAPLAN CFP Exam Required Education Course 2018."

The initial design of MPI™ was purely scientific, absent of emotion, depending upon math to tell the story—a design that could push your risk lower on the Pyramid while increasing your potential long-term returns. That process lead to features and benefits that enhanced compounding effects while staying true to the Exponential Growth formula.

When I finished MPI™, it was not received very well. As I mentioned in Chapter 6, many, including brokers, financial advisors, actuaries, and attorneys told me this concept would never work. They said there was no way security and increased growth could co-exist. But when I provided the math, research, historical data, back testing, cost analysis, and all other details of MPI™ to prove how it would satisfy the criteria of a viable financial plan ready to take to the public, people listened and soon realized that this was possible by holding security as an enduring principle.

The 0% Floor provided by the General Fund was the ultimate feature that provided the rock-foundation for everything else to work in unison. The evolution that had taken place through addressing each concern gave birth to a version of MPI™ approved for the public in 2018. Its evolution continues as my experience accumulates and client feedback is taken into consideration. And it continues to evolve and grow, always seeking additional advancements for the best long-term success.

Inside MPI™, there are 10 features working in balance. Removing any one feature reduces the potential of optimal results within the financial plan. No one feature dominates another as they all work in harmony to eliminate risk and avoid the flawed approach of diversification, an approach that accepts loss as part of the process.

To be fully transparent, the creative process to develop and build the MPI™ system represents a six-year period, thousands of hours of research, testing and adjusting, and a labor of love to deliver the world the Science of Compound Interest. The MPI™ plan is currently patent pending as my mission continues to bring value, education, and solutions that make money more efficient and effective regardless of the demographic.

When someone starts down the path of MPI™, I earn income because this is my source of living. Following the publication of my first book, *Everyone Ends Up Poor!*, a few reviews suggested that my only motivation was to "sell insurance and make a buck."

My response is that I seek to provide value, which, in this case, takes the form of an insurance contract, one that is customized to the best of my ability to reflect the success equation of Exponential Growth and is completely transparent in its mechanics. MPI™ is my answer to financial well-being, accessible to as many people as possible, with the sole intention of benefiting those people.

You should be aware of the fact that I am both the inventor AND a client of MPI™. This is the plan I built for myself and my family.

As I further explain the features of MPI™, you will come to realize that making money is an outcome of the value I deliver, not a goal in and of itself. Now let's look at those 10 features and benefits of MPI™ mentioned previously and how you win with them!

1. MPI™ is permanent life insurance, meaning it has no expiration date. Unlike term insurance, it is 100% guaranteed to pay out to my wife, kids, or whomever I choose when I pass away, as long as the policy remains in force. This guarantees that no matter my age at death, generational wealth is achieved. Various financial influencers suggest permanent insurance is "expensive" and advise to "buy term, invest the rest" as a more cost-effective strategy. However, that bogus philosophy is also falsely premised on the condition that by the time we are 65, we are self-insured. I know many people, and few of them fall into a category of financial prosperity at death, much less during life. "Buy term, invest the rest" is a short-sighted, linear approach to financial security. Though the cost of insurance does increase over time, the compounding mechanism outpaces the natural effect of inflation. It's never about how much you pay, but how much you grow.

2. MPI™ has a feature called Living Benefits. If you were to get sick with chronic or terminal illness, you can withdraw an advance on your life insurance to pay for qualified medical expenses. This protects families from financial devastation stemming from health scares such as cancer, heart attack, stroke, and various other severe illnesses. Many have a family member who has had a frightening medical diagnosis, myself included. My wife was diagnosed with cancer in 2011, bringing to bear a very trying time, incurring mounds of medical bills in the process. Thankfully, the evolution of modern medicine prevailed, and she has been cancer-free for seven years as of this writing. Though my business was producing enough income to cover all the medical expenses, that is an anomaly. Most families in our country are not so blessed. That is why inside the MPI™ plan, no matter your income level, if you were to get this illness, you would have access to this benefit to cover excessive medical bills, thereby preserving the house you built on the ROCK.

3. MPI™ is designed with the intent of keeping net expenses as low as possible. Lower net expenses mean more money in secure growth, more money available to leverage, and an increased compounding effect. This specific life insurance design is what I call a **Max-Funded, Option B, Indexed Universal Life.** This choice removes most of the up-front expenses of an Option A IUL or Whole Life policy. It is rarely used by insurance agents, probably because it substantially lowers commissions. If you have a Cash Value life insurance plan and it is not a Max-Funded, Option B, it will likely underperform as a retirement plan.

The fees inside of a **Max-Funded, Option B, IUL** are often misunderstood and misrepresented. Various financial influencers claim that "cash value life insurance" is overly expensive. But is it really? I've shown the math validating the expense of traditional plans, such as the 401(k), and now I will explain the fee structure of an MPI™ plan.

An MPI™ plan is built inside a structure called "Linear Fees" rather than "Compounding Fees" I touched on this important distinction in Chapter 2. Rather than charge a percentage of the account value within the plan (i.e. compounding fees growing at the same rate as your account), the insurance company charges a percentage of annual contribution into the plan. This method of fees is also referred to as a "Front-End Load" fee because fees are charged on what you put in rather than the gains.

"Front-End Load" fees have a tremendous advantage in long-term planning, though they are not as helpful in short-term planning. Again, we are fighting our biology because one plan feels good today, while the other plan feels good in the future. Here are the projected fees inside of a Max-Funded, Option B, IUL for a 25-year-old male contributing $10,000 a year into his plan:

MAX-FUNDED OPTION B IUL FEES

AGE	ANNUAL CONTRIBUTION	ANNUAL POLICY FEE	CUMULATIVE FEES	PROJECTED ACCOUNT VALUE	% OF ACCOUNT VALUE
25	$10,000	$1,105	$1,105	$9,104	12.14%
29			$5,525	$40,408	2.73%
30		$555	$6,080	$52,280	1.06%
34			$8,300	$127,584	0.44%
35		$417	$8,717	$145,754	0.29%
45			$12,887	$404,595	0.10%
55			$17,057	$887,588	0.047%
65			$21,227	$1,782,666	0.023%
70	$0	$60	$21,527	$2,479,132	0.0024%
80			$22,127	$4,652,581	0.0013%
90			**$22,727**	**$8,332,481**	**0.00072%**

*Fees Projected From an NAIC Approved Illustration For a 25-Year-Old-Male, Standard Health Rating. *Fees Projected From an NAIC Approved Illustration For a 25-Year-Old Standard Health. *Contributions Stopped at 65 Years Old. *Account Value Estimate Based on a 6.54% Annual Return. *Projections Do Not Include MPI™ Leverage Feature.

As you can see, the fees are significant in the first five years; they taper off during the next five years and ultimately flatline. Ranging from 10 to 12% of contribution amount out of the gate, reducing to around 5–6% and finishing around 4–5%, all of which are linear because of being attached solely to the amount contributed to the plan.

Let's look at an apples-to-apples comparison to traditional plans that charge a compounding 1% fee of the account value. If our fee percentage were represented based on the MPI™ account value instead of the contribution, the percentage drops from around 11% to as low as 0.0007% annually in later years.

This is the power of linear fees so that when you need your money to be compounding the most in the later years, the fees are the lowest possible, yet another example of speeding up cycles. Traditional risk-based plans produce a *linear result with compounding fees* where MPI™ focus is exactly opposite, *compounding results with linear fees*. Traditional plans prioritize their fees whereas MPI™ prioritizes **your success**!

LINEAR VS COMPOUNDING FEES

AGE	IUL CUMULATIVE FEES	401(K) CUMULATIVE FEES	DIFFERENCE
25	$1,105	$110	$995
35	$8,717	$9,950	$1,233
45	$12,887	$49,956	$37,069
55	$17,057	$156,150	$139,093
65	$21,227	$370,864	$349,637
70	$21,527	$436,022	$414,495
80	$22,127	$549,655	$527,528
90	$22,727	$612,233	$589,506

*Fees Projected From an NAIC Approved Illustration For a 25-Year-Old-Male, Standard Health Rating. *Contributions Stopped at 65 Years Old. *Account Value Estimate Based on a 6.54% Annual Return For the IUL. *Projections For the 401(K) Estimated From Sprint, Run, Jog, Walk Returns With a 1% Management Fee, and 0.5% Management Fee During Retirement.

Option B has one additional benefit. Many financial gurus state that inside of cash value life insurance, when you pass away, your beneficiary will get either your cash value or the life insurance, whichever is greater in value.

This is true for Option A, which is called "Level Death Benefit"; however, Option B is called "Increasing Death Benefit," which means along with your life insurance value, every dollar you add to the account increases your death benefit payout. When you pass away, your beneficiary gets both the life insurance AND the cash value.

This compounding-focused design provides the absolute lowest costs of any financial plan I've found in the entire financial industry, including that of a self-managed index fund, over the life of a retirement plan. Even the well-intentioned rarely use this plan due to a lack of understanding.

4. MPI™ is based on tax-code §7702(a). Although §401(k) offers great immediate tax advantages, further research indicates that §7702(a) provides even better tax advantages for long-term wealth accumulation and legacy planning. MPI™ is a post-tax system (as is the Roth IRA) meaning funding is from money on which you've already paid tax. Because funding is with post-

tax dollars, the code allows all MPI™ distributions and retirement income to be distributed 100% tax-free, free from capital gains tax on all the compounding growth of your money, and 100% tax-free transfer to your beneficiary. At present, this is the most tax efficient vehicle I have found.

5. MPI™ is one of the most legislatively protected assets from lawsuits, liens, creditors, or judgements. Though state-law governs insurance, most provide legislative protection, making it difficult to sue a life insurance plan. For business owners, the threat of a lawsuit is always on our minds because what we have taken years to build could be taken in a blink of an eye.

6. MPI™ has no age restrictions for retirement income or distributions. Retirement day is the day you decide and has nothing to do with an arbitrary age or formula, as there are no penalties to access your money. This is quite unlike a §401(k), IRA, or pension, all of which have restrictions, limitations, and penalties to access retirement funds before age 59 ½ (or another age by formula, tax-code condition, etc.), adding a 10% penalty to any distribution taken. MPI™ has no such strings attached to your money. This feature is crucial to the MPI™ plan because without it, we could not add the leverage component of the equation. Cause and effect dictate that one little benefit can snowball into compounding rewards.

7. MPI™ incorporates the Yin of investing (security) by using the General Fund of the life insurance company. This feature provides guaranteed security for your money. I have yet to find an asset that provides guaranteed security plus growth above the rate-of-inflation other than a cash value life insurance plan. In MPI™ we call this the 0% Floor, a contractual guarantee that during a market downturn of any magnitude, you will NEVER earn less than 0%. In my first book, *Everyone Ends Up Poor!*, I call the 0% Floor the Ultimate Feature because without this guaranteed

security, Compound Interest cannot be optimized, Compound Cycles will be delayed in any downturns, and the NET result in your lifetime could be millions of dollars less. Many have experienced what I'm referring to as your account "recovered" after a market downturn, taking years just to get back to even.

8. MPI™ is built inside of the Yang of investing (growth) by using the Call Option strategy on the S&P 500 Index. By mitigating the volatility risk with this strategy (using only the growth of the General Fund for the Call Option), instead of claiming to do the same by "diversifying," we have a path to achieve security and strong growth potential simultaneously. Yin and Yang, seemingly opposite forces, work together to produce the best result. At the time of this writing, there is a ceiling of growth-potential, between 10–15% of the S&P 500 Index returns (without dividends), proving singles and doubles outperform home runs and strikeouts over a long period of time. "Moneyball" inside of finances!

Throughout the past 20 years of tremendous volatility, the IUL has produced around 7–8% actual return, significantly more than an S&P 500 Index Fund (with dividends). Many advisors caution to "watch out for IUL's, they can change the caps on you any time they want" or "you have to give up the big Index return years." They are correct, yet that is merely one chapter in a long novel. As mentioned, hitting singles and doubles is the goal, as long as we never strikeout. The foregone value of the home run is not worth the long-term risk (damage) that a strikeout represents. Also, the cap may change, not out of some weirdly malicious or greedy intention, but based on the long-term returns of the General Fund. We are all impacted by the same market and by how much benefit the Call Option strategy brings. Market returns and these fluctuations affect everyone. However, no matter the cap, we benefit most by the 0% Floor, which protects the ability to compound without "rebounds."

9. The feature that sets MPI™ apart from anything the financial world has ever produced: Secure Leverage. Not only is Secure Leverage a rare feat but is now available to anyone, not just the wealthy with good credit. Through the capped Participating Loan offered by the life insurance company, you can increase the amount of money earning Compound Interest. The leveraged money isn't yours, but you get to keep the interest it earns for you in the same way that you may have a mortgage from a bank, but the increase in your home value is all yours.

   You can also compare the MPI™ benefits to a match program like the $401(k) but rather than matching your contribution in a broken system, the insurance company provides leverage features you can use to increase your Compound Interest within a secure, efficient system. This method of increasing Compound Cycles, rather than focusing solely on increasing dollars, has proven to be more valuable to your future. This Participating Loan, unlike traditional loans, is always dollar-for-dollar collateralized; therefore, it is not a liability to pay back. It is a permanent loan that will be paid back when you pass away. It doesn't require a credit check, origination fees, commissions to be paid, etc. Because this loan typically charges between 4–6%, and thanks to our General Fund + Call Option strategy that has produced an average of 7–8% historically, it provides a net benefit used to accelerate your Compound Interest. It also provides the path to becoming a Pure Compounder, continuing to make money after you spend it (see the previous chapter). Because life insurance distributions (money you will spend) are also a Participating Loan, they are 100% tax-free, but, more importantly, these distributions preserve your money so it can continue to grow at around 7–8% on average, while you are paying only 4–6% for the "loan." Always remind yourself that you win when Interest Earned is greater than Interest Paid!

10. Lastly, why are we willing to sacrifice and save money when *You Only Live Once* sounds inspirational? Financial freedom and abundance! Retirement income! The ability to do what we want, when we want, and with whom we want is possible with MPI™ when the previous 9

components work together. This concurrent teamwork increases retirement income by up to 4x compared to a traditional plan using 401(k), IRA, real estate, and all mainstream retirement accounts predicated on the 4% Rule of distribution. Does MPI™ produce a 4x bigger nest egg than a 401(k)? The answer is no, because the size of your nest egg isn't the driving force behind retirement income. However, rate of return in your later years is! Because MPI™ applies the theory of Jog, Run, and then Sprint, it is designed to maximize retirement income. It all goes back to "risk." When a portfolio is built with risk, tapering off in the later years is a requirement, cutting your rate of return dramatically. Because of the 0% Floor security, MPI™ is never required to taper off from its growth strategy, and when you add the Secure Leverage, the Compound Interest gradually increases to a full sprint and maintains that speed throughout retirement. MPI™, depending on how long leverage can mature, can produce up to 16% income in retirement, outproducing "The 4% Rule" by up to 400%.

TRADITIONAL RETIREMENT INCOME

RISK-BASED	AGE	RATE OF RETURN
SPRINT	20s-40s	8-12%
RUN	50s-60s	6-8%
JOG	60s+	4-6%
WALK	RETIREMENT	3-5%

4% SAFE RETIREMENT INCOME POTENTIAL

MPI™ RETIREMENT INCOME

SECURE LEVERAGE	TIME	RATE OF RETURN
JOG	YEARS 1-9	8-10%
RUN	YEARS 10-19	10-12%
SPRINT	YEARS 20+	12%+

12%+ SAFE RETIREMENT INCOME POTENTIAL

*Longer Maturity Inside MPI™ Increases Retirement Income.

An increase of up to 400% is no small claim. The MPI™ platform, built on the science of secure Compound Cycles rather than an insecure exciting rate of return, provides for the absolute best future, focused on eliminating stress, anxiety, and worries about risk, taxes, sufficient income, legacy planning, retirement age, and all the other problematic aspects of traditional financial planning.

Imagine starting a financial plan at 21 and being able to retire at 45? Or starting one for a newborn, and having no concern of financial stress in their adulthood? How much value does that bring to someone's life? Your life? Or saving a lot and retiring in less than 10 years? Many people say to me "but what if I don't want to retire?"

Retirement shouldn't be the goal of "not working," but the freedom to do whatever you want with your time. Continue to work if you like, start a non-profit, or go on a religious mission. You will be able to make the decisions that fit your lifestyle because you are financially free; that is a state nearly impossible to achieve in the traditional retirement system fueled by: 401(k)/IRA/real estate rentals.

This is not just my work, it's my legacy.

When I meet individuals and families, I am often asked "what does it take to retire?" Within the MPI™ system, based upon historical returns over the last 90 years, it's both predictable and simple to determine the amount of money and time it should take to achieve your goals. Obviously, no one can predict the future, but using the data we have, we can build a pretty accurate plan for you to achieve the retirement you want.

Because MPI™ is built upon $y = a(1 + r)^x$, with slow, steady, and secure growth, the only variables for which you are responsible are **(a)** and **(1)**. How much money do you put into it and for how long? **(+)**, **(r)**, and **(x)** are consistent in the MPI™ system and managed by the insurance company. We know we can't lose value inside the General Fund, we know we will achieve around 7% interest on average (0%-11% floor-ceiling strategy) inside the S&P 500 Call Option strategy over the 20 years of returns (and back-tested over the last 90 years of returns), and we know we can leverage according to the cash value inside our account.

So, what does it take to retire? What is your goal? The most common goal that I hear from individuals is to retire with $100,000 tax-free income.

You can live an amazing life with $100,000 of tax-free annual spendable income. By using the equation, here is what would be needed to achieve this retirement.

$100,000 TAX-FREE RETIREMENT INCOME

ANNUAL CONTRIBUTION	YEARS	ESTIMATED RETIREMENT INCOME
$500,000	2	
$300,000	3	
$175,000	5	
$100,000	8	
$50,000	12	**$100,000** ANNUALLY FOR LIFE
$30,000	15	
$20,000	20	
$10,000	25	
$5,000	30	
$2,500	40	

*MPI™ Results Calculated From 2005-2019 S&P 500 Returns Repeated. **Fees Projected From an NAIC Approved Illustration 35 Year-Old- Preferred Health Rating Male. *0% Floor, 11% Cap Used to Calculate Returns. *Income Tax-Free Increased Annual For Inflation.

Do you want $200,000 of retirement income? Then double the contribution amounts for the same time period or allow more time to achieve one additional Compound Cycle! $50,000? Cut your contributions in half. It's a math equation! Think about how amazing that is. If you make a lot of money and desire to build a secure retirement account; you can do so in less than 10 years. If you make a little less but can save $2,500–$5,000 a year? You can build an amazing retirement in 30–40 years. MPI™ is a path for everyone to achieve the freedom they desire.

Another way to think about retirement goals is retiring on "full income." The accomplishment of making the same paycheck in retirement as when you were working full time. Using the same data as above, the following chart provides the percentage of annual savings and estimated timeframe needed to have a full income retirement.

As you can see, some goals would require over 100% savings, which is not possible, but can be accomplished by using other savings and assets to accelerate your MPI™ account.

"FULL INCOME" TAX-FREE RETIREMENT

ANNUAL CONTRIBUTION	YEARS	ESTIMATED RETIREMENT INCOME
500%	2	
300%	3	
175%	5	
100%	8	
50%	12	**FULL INCOME**
30%	15	**ANNUALLY FOR LIFE**
20%	20	
10%	25	
5%	30	
2.5%	40	

*MPI™ Results Calculated From 2005-2019 S&P 500 Returns Repeated. *Fees Projected From an NAIC Approved Illustration For a 35 Year-Old Male, Preferred Health Rating. *0% Floor, 11% Cap Used to Calculate Returns. *Income Tax-Free Increased Annual For Inflation.

Is the voice in your head saying, "This is too good to be true"? It checks off every box we would ever want within one financial vehicle, aside from the one labeled "get rich quick." There is no such thing as getting rich quick, easy money, or overnight success without tremendous risk.

However, there is: life insurance, living benefits, low cost, tax advantages, legal protection, no restrictions or penalties on distribution, no risk in the stock market, a good Compound Interest, liquidity for emergency money, plus leveragability using O.P.M. (Other People's Money) to speed up growth, all in plain sight as a cash value life insurance max-funded, Option B IUL.

And to top it all off, increased income by up to 400% in retirement over your current 401(k)/IRA/real estate rentals! But when you add all these features together in an optimal design, the math is undeniable. The claim is undebatable because it is built on the "Rock" and stands firm when the rains come down.

As you begin to understand the science behind MPI™ and how it is the only financial plan available that balances the demands of Compound Interest, the common question "how much do I have to put in?" transforms to "how much **CAN** I put in?" At that moment, you've bridged the gap between the linear and exponential mindset, beginning your path to become a Pure Compounder.

Can one financial plan really be this good? The answer is yes, though it is not perfect. There are five drawbacks to MPI™ for which I have not yet found a solution, though we continue to look to evolution to solve them (but as of now, the benefits substantially outweigh the drawbacks):

1. *Surrender Charge.* Within MPI™, the first-year contribution (varies depending on age and policy details) to your policy can be ear-marked as a "Surrender Charge" or cancellation penalty. The insurance company incurs expenses to set up these advanced plans, so to protect their investment in what is designed as a lifelong plan, they place a lien on a percentage of your initial premiums. The money is still in your account compounding for you, though not all of it may be available to leverage or withdraw. If you were to make the linear, short-term decision to cancel the plan, the insurance company would keep the amount designated as the surrender lien to cover their expenses. Each year you are in the system, they release a portion of the lien until 100% of it is available to you. Surrender Charge has no effect on your compounding unless you cancel the plan. Most insurance companies have a declining Surrender Charge Period ranging 9–14 years. After that, there is no penalty to cancel. Below is an example of a Surrender Charge schedule for someone who contributes $10,000 in the first year of their MPI™ plan. With a $5,000 first year contribution, the surrender charge would be around half (a $20,000 first year contribution would be around double).

SURRENDER CHARGE SCHEDULE

YEAR	CANCELLATION PENALTY
1	$8,562
2	$8,206
3	$7,492
4	$6,778
5	$6,065
6	$5,351
7	$4,638
8	$3,924
9	$3,568
10	$3,211
11	$2,497
12	$1,784
13	$1,070
14	$357
15	$0

*Surrender Charges Taken From an NAIC Approved Illustration For a 35-Year-Old Male, Preferred Health Rating. *Based on an Annual Premium of $10,000.

2. *Cost of Insurance (COI)*. Inside of the MPI™ system, the COI is built on a concept called Annual Renewable Term (ART). This type of insurance varies in cost every year according to your age. As you get older, the cost traditionally increases. This is a huge drawback to the traditional IUL that MPI™ solves. Because we typically earn an additional 3% interest on average in Secure Leverage, this additional gain offsets the increase in COI while

also speeding up the compounding. This allows for us to eliminate the risk of insurance becoming too expensive as we get older because compounding outpaces the increase in COI. Here is an example of ART for a healthy male, 35 years old, contributing $10,000 into his MPI™ until 85 years old.

35-85 YEAR OLD COST OF INSURANCE (ART)

$10,000 ANNUAL CONTRIBUTION / $356,761 INSURANCE POLICY

AGE	ANNUAL COST OF INSURANCE	ANNUAL NET INTEREST EARNED	PERCENT OF GROWTH
35	$217	-$408	-53.15%
40	$345	$3,501	9.85%
45	$441	$12,156	3.63%
50	$550	$30,043	1.83%
55	$830	$56,585	1.47%
60	$1,172	$93,088	1.26%
65	$1,978	$143,239	1.38%
70	$3,301	$214,306	1.54%
75	$6,072	$307,637	1.97%
80	$10,961	$426,421	2.57%
85	$20,725	$574,360	3.61%
TOTALS	**$185,726**	**$8,090,205**	**2.30%**

*COI Estimated Cost Taken From a 2019 NAIC Approved Illustration for a 35-Year-Old Male Preferred Plus Health Rating. *Based on an Annual Premium of $10,000. *Based on a 6.8% Annual Returns. *Based on a Permanent Life Insurance Policy of $356,761. *Assumed 4% Loan Rate for the MPI™ Secure Leverage Feature.

The Max-funded Option B required insurance amount would be around $350,000 and total lifetime costs estimated at $185,726 by age 85. Through focusing on compounding, you can see the ART expense is a very small percentage of around 2% of the total estimated lifetime NET interest earned. When the mainstream financial gurus claim the insurance cost of a cash value life insurance will eat up most of your growth as you get older, they have little understanding how the COI annual increase affects the Compound Interest potential in an MPI™ account.

3. *Leverage Qualifications.* The MPI™ system does not begin to leverage right out of the gate. Because the initial premiums are largely designated as a "Surrender Charge," there isn't much liquidity to leverage after only one year. Because "Surrender" usually applies to the first-year contribution, subsequent contributions gradually provide liquidity and leveragability in your account. Leverage takes time to mature, however once we begin, MPI™ optimizes the leveragability of your money.

4. *Bond Markets.* The General Fund of the insurance company is mostly comprised of secure Bonds and secure mortgage notes. This is the source of income used to purchase the Call Option Spread. At the time of this writing and for some time previous, the Bond market is at historic lows; it could go even lower or may move higher—no one can know. This movement affects the caps within MPI™. For example, if Bond yields increase, more money is being earned by the General Fund allowing a greater amount to be allotted to the Call Options, potentially increasing the caps.

5. *Long-term Stagnant Markets.* MPI™ flourishes in the chaos of volatility. Because MPI™ eliminates the risk of the market from the equation, huge crashes like the Great Recession, dotcom or even the Great Depression have little effect on the success of MPI™. What would influence MPI™ is market returns between 0 and 5% every year for a long period. In this scenario, leverage would not have a positive effect on our account. Thankfully, history is on our side: since the Great Depression, the stock market has never

had a long-term stagnant market. That is not how the market behaves. Peaks and valleys are nearly guaranteed in the world in which we live. It goes up, and it goes down, and this provides the best environment for MPI™ to flourish.

How secure is the MPI™ Leverage system?

Not only has it produced heightened results in the current market environment (the past 20 years), but back-testing using actual stock market returns dating to the Great Depression, reveals a 100% success rate in producing significantly better results over all other available (traditional) solutions. MPI™ won every single time.

Let me clarify this statement with greater detail. I have run thousands of simulations of rolling periods of actual returns from 1929 to 2019, including a variety of stock/bond portfolios, various Index Funds, rental real estate, Whole Life, IULs, and VULs. In all cases, MPI™ produced significantly more retirement income over the competition. It never lost. I understand the magnitude of this declaration; however, it is based in math and science rather than speculation and hype. And this means it can be reproduced, so I am confident to make such statements. Nothing is perfect, but when compared to the available options, MPI™ provides the highest probability of success with maximized retirement income.

Therefore, I opened my own MPI™ plan focused on secure compounding. When designed correctly as a Max-Funded, Option B, IUL (something even seasoned life insurance agents and financial advisors don't fully understand), there is nothing like it.

In my 15 years of business and investing experience, I've been introduced to almost every type of investment (putting my own money in almost all of them that seemed like good opportunities). And only by becoming educated on the science of compounding done correctly, according to $y = a(1 + r)^x$, have I gained complete confidence that within MPI™, my money has the most potential to produce wealth, security, and freedom for me and my family!

MPI™ FINANCIAL PLAN

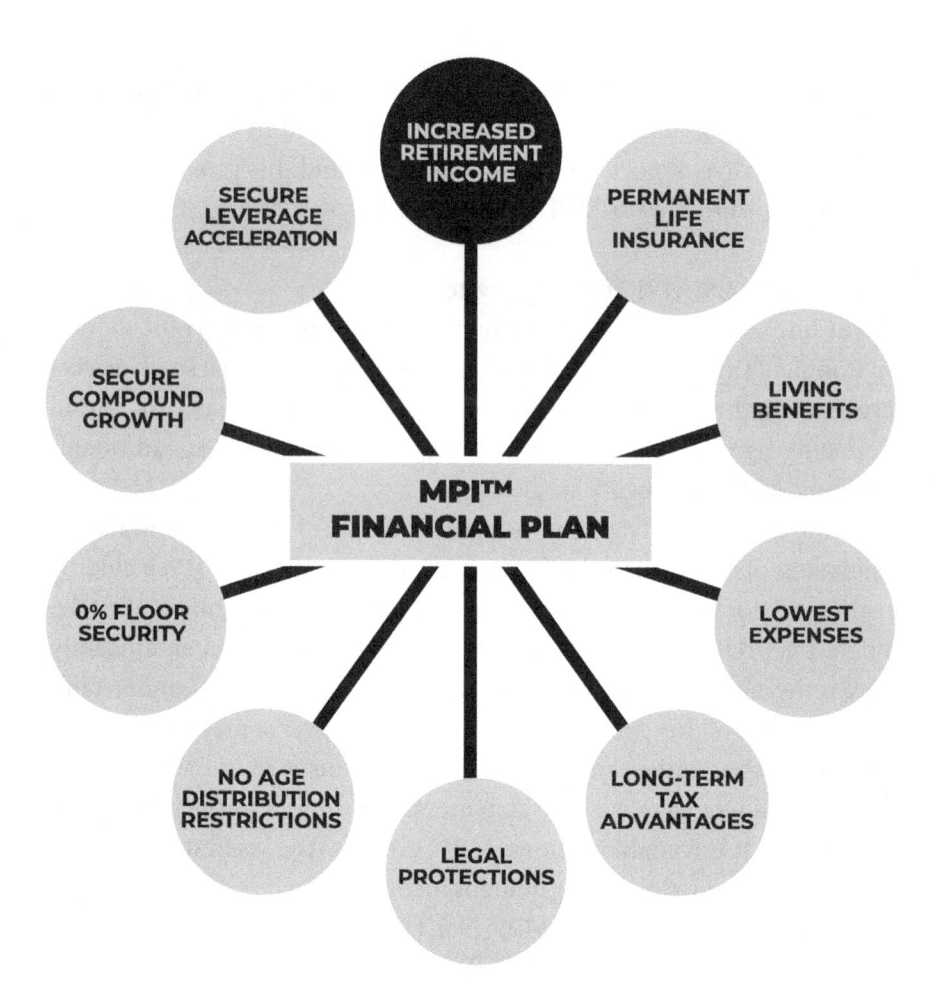

- INCREASED RETIREMENT INCOME
- PERMANENT LIFE INSURANCE
- LIVING BENEFITS
- LOWEST EXPENSES
- LONG-TERM TAX ADVANTAGES
- LEGAL PROTECTIONS
- NO AGE DISTRIBUTION RESTRICTIONS
- 0% FLOOR SECURITY
- SECURE COMPOUND GROWTH
- SECURE LEVERAGE ACCELERATION

"Greatness is not a function of circumstance. Greatness, it turns out, is largely a matter of conscious choice, and discipline."

Jim Collins

NOTES/THOUGHTS

CHAPTER 10
MPI™ to the Test

It all sounds good in theory, but does it work in real-life scenarios? Is "Always Be Compounding" really what is best for everyone, every single time: the true secret to maximize freedom in your life? I claim that one size doesn't fit all, but all sizes fit one: SECURE COMPOUNDING!

Let's put it to the test and see how the math compares against common "advice" we receive from the "trusted" financial gurus. Below are a variety of scenarios using the ABC of Wealth to analyze how each scenario fared using MPI™ compared to the status quo. Buckle up as this will get bumpy!

S&P 500 INDEX FUND WITH DIVIDENDS

Warren Buffett wrote in the Berkshire Hathaway 2016 annual shareholder letter, "My regular recommendation has been a low-cost S&P 500 Index Fund." Since 1975, since the birth of the Index Fund, it has been one of most consistently producing investment accounts available to the public. Not only is it one of the lowest expense accounts, it has consistently outperformed the traditional money manager around 80% of the time.

The S&P 500 Index Fund is recommended across the board by nearly every financial influencer. As mentioned, there is one major flaw to it. Even with all its advantages, it still lives inside (+/-). It has great home run potential, it can outproduce a Secure Compound Interest account in the early years, but can it outproduce secure compounding over a 30-year retirement plan?

Taking the actual returns from 1990–2019 of the S&P 500 Index Fund with dividends, with the various home runs and strikeouts of the last three decades versus the slow, steady, and secure method of MPI™ that has a 0% Floor Security and an 11% Cap, what would have been the outcome? One is focused on the rate of return and lowest expenses while the other focused on rate of compounding and acceleration of cycles. Here are the results of the last 30 years head to head.

1990-2019 S&P 500 WITH DIVIDENDS VS MPI™
$500 MONTHLY CONTRIBUTION FOR 30 YEARS

YEAR	AGE	S&P 500 RETURNS	ACCOUNT CASH VALUE	MPI™ RETURNS	ACCOUNT CASH VALUE
1989	24	-	$0	-	$0
1990	25	-3.42%	$5,790	0.0%	$5,323
1991	26	30.95%	$14,880	11.0%	$11,803
1992	27	7.60%	$21,446	4.76%	$18,582
1993	28	10.17%	$29,056	7.45%	$26,952
1994	29	1.19%	$35,135	0.0%	$31,038
1995	30	38.02%	$54,030	11.0%	$42,694
1996	31	23.06%	$72,368	11.0%	$56,620
1997	32	33.67%	$100,306	11.0%	$73,451
1998	33	28.73%	$132,940	11.0%	$93,603
1999	34	21.11%	$162,914	11.0%	$117,863
2000	35	-9.11%	$153,950	0.0%	$116,089
2001	36	-11.98%	$141,394	0.0%	$112,883
2002	37	-22.27%	$115,814	0.0%	$108,153
2003	38	28.72%	$150,995	11.0%	$144,130
2004	39	10.82%	$168,616	8.99%	$177,502
2005	40	4.79%	$178,151	3.0%	$183,815
2006	41	15.74%	$214,327	11.0%	$236,555
2007	42	5.46%	$234,716	3.53%	$247,258
2008	43	-37.22%	$153,234	0.0%	$231,901
2009	44	27.11%	$203,485	11.0%	$299,266
2010	45	14.87%	$244,471	11.0%	$377,341
2011	46	2.07%	$250,083	0.0%	$355,393
2012	47	15.88%	$293,013	11.0%	$446,721
2013	48	32.43%	$392,467	11.0%	$551,895
2014	49	13.81%	$447,960	11.0%	$672,573
2015	50	1.31%	$457,657	0.0%	$640,690
2016	51	11.93%	$531,269	9.54%	$756,284
2017	52	21.94%	$646,835	11.0%	$911,839
2018	53	-4.42%	$623,746	0.0%	$870,956
2019	54	31.49%	$828,373	11.0%	$1,047,902
TOTAL	-	**9.88%**	**$828,373**	**7.0%**	**$1,047,902**
ANNUAL RETIREMENT @AGE 55		**4% INCOME**	**$33,135**	**12% INCOME**	**$125,748**

Results Calculated Using the 1990-2019 S&P 500 Index Returns with Dividends Reinvested With an Expense Ratio of .08% and MPI™ Using a 0% Floor and 11% Cap S&P 500 Crediting Without Dividends. Projections Based on a 25-Year-Old Male with Preferred Health, Saving $6000 Annually for 30 Years, Retiring at 55 Years Old. Capital Gains Tax Assumed At 15% On Gains Inside the S&P 500 Index Fund.

From these actual 30-year returns, we can see the S&P 500 Index Fund had a geometric average of over 9.88% where MPI™ only averaged 7%.

With the great performance of the 1990's, an S&P 500 Index Fund produced more account cash value than MPI™ out of the gate.

But once MPI™ began to mature through Secure Leverage, increasing the number of buckets producing Secure Compound Interest, and not taking the catastrophic effects of the down markets of the 2000's, MPI™ would have outproduced the world's most recommended investment account by up to 20% account cash value. However, that's just one part of the story.

Because MPI™ is not built to slow down like nearly all other retirement investment accounts, it can produce over $125,000 of annual retirement income while the S&P 500 Index Fund, built inside the risk-based theory of the 4% Rule (Sprint, Run, Jog, Walk), would produce an underwhelming retirement income of around $33,000.

Nearly a 400% increase in income by understanding the universal laws of compounding and security. These enhanced results don't even take into consideration all the other features and benefits of MPI™ including life insurance, tax advantages, and various others.

MPI™ > S&P 500 Index Fund

INDEXED UNIVERSAL LIFE

The strange part of my journey over the last five years has been the opposition I have experienced from the insurance world in general. Agents across the country want to argue about why their Indexed Universal Life/Whole life is best in the market and why MPI™ will not work. They often claim that the leverage feature cannot make additional interest because the loan rate and cost of insurance will exhaust all additional gains. What is even stranger is the fact that these same agents and insurance influencers will make videos on how the loan feature within the policy should be used during retirement years to maintain "participation" and gain the additional interest spread. They promote the benefits of always using the loan feature for tax-free retirement income while continuing the compounding of your money, which is all true.

When I introduce them to the idea that if you can make a spread on the loan feature, why would we wait until age 65 to use it? Why not begin immediately and accelerate the compounding potential, especially when the cost of insurance is so low? The loan feature has more value the earlier you start using it! But even the open-minded insurance world struggles with the linear mind and breaking out of the "this is how it has always been done" mentality.

For decades, the insurance world has used the loan feature to pay off debt, generate tax-free retirement income, provide liquidity, and various other advantages, but had never considered or checked the math of using the loan to accelerate and enhance the growth potential internally, at the policy level. And when I do present this concept to various financial companies of enhanced Secure Compounding, few take the time to check my math and validate the claims I make, telling me they are happy with their current system.

The sad reality is that because of this mentality and comfort level, client's across the country will be the ones missing out on significantly more retirement income and death benefit for their family.

Here is a side-by-side of a Max-funded, Option B Indexed Universal Life (the most efficient and lowest cost IUL) vs the same plan but enhanced with the MPI™ Secure Leverage feature.

\multicolumn{3}{c	}{INDEXED UNIVERSAL LIFE}	\multicolumn{3}{c}{MPI™}
\multicolumn{6}{c}{$10,000 ANNUAL CONTRIBUTION}
AGE	ESTIMATED CASH VALUE	ANNUAL RETIREMENT INCOME	AGE	ESTIMATED CASH VALUE	ANNUAL RETIREMENT INCOME
35	$9,592		35	$9,592	
40	$67,270		40	$67,585	
45	$148,712	—	45	$166,182	—
50	$262,326		50	$340,485	
55	$418,923		55	$633,364	
60	$634,659		60	$1,091,403	
65	$861,686	$69,113	65	$1,580,557	$193,931
70	$854,880	$76,306	70	$1,424,549	$214,115
75	$862,534	$84,248	75	$1,328,820	$236,401
80	$897,615	$93,017	80	$1,328,064	$261,005
85	$972,911	$102,698	85	$1,444,614	$288,171
TOTAL	$972,911	$1,781,962	TOTAL	$1,444,614	$5,000,182

*Estimated Costs Taken From a 2019 NAIC Approved Illustration for a 35-Year-Old Male Preferred Health Rating. *Based on an Annual Premium of $10,000. *Based on a 6.8% Annual Returns. *Assumed 4% Loan Rate for the MPI™ Secure Leverage Feature. *Annual Income Increased for Inflation.

Same plan, same contributions, same person, in the same amount of time... and the results? Up to 3x the retirement income through Secure Leverage!

MPI™ > Indexed Universal Life

PAY DOWN YOUR MORTGAGE AS QUICKLY AS POSSIBLE

Paying off your mortgage as soon as possible is common advice given by experts as essential to the quest for financial security and freedom. By now, you know I will point out the flaw that this strategy promotes: By early payment of your mortgage, you're giving your hard-earned money to the bank and allowing them (instead of you) to secure, compound, and leverage your money. You save pennies in interest while they make dollars.

A misconception and false teaching we are often told is that mortgage interest is Compound Interest.

It is not! Most debt, assuming that you make your minimum payment, is what is termed "simple interest." Compound Interest is when both the principal and additional interest are added together, causing an increase in principal value; you earn an increase in interest from the new higher value; that is the meaning of "compounding."

This is not the case with mortgages, or even credit cards. If you pay at least the interest, if not the minimum payment, the balance does not increase.

Let's break it down and see what effect this has on your lifetime wealth. The example we will use is someone who buys their first house at age 30 with the goal to pay it off in 10 years. After the house is paid off, what had been the payment amount are then contributed to MPI™ from age 40–60. What is the compounding potential in their lifetime (to age 90)?

Compare this to someone using the MPI™ plan. They pay the minimum on their mortgage for 30 years, while compounding the difference (the *extra* part of the payment needed if they were paying off the loan in 10 years) into MPI™ during the term of the loan (to age 60). They then cease contributing into MPI™ and allow the money to continue to compound to age 90. Both scenarios are the identical amount of money out of pocket. The difference is how much time it had to compound.

10 YEAR MORTGAGE PAYOFF FOCUS *BEFORE* MPI™

AGE	MORTGAGE MONTHLY PAYMENT	MPI™ MONTHLY CONTRIBUTION	MPI™ ACCOUNT VALUE	ANNUAL RETIREMENT INCOME
30	$3,037	$0	$0	$0
35				
40	$0	$3,037	$0	
45			$188,000	
50			$615,000	
55			$1,172,000	
60	$0	$0	$1,907,000	$209,770
70			$2,886,000	$250,695
80			$4,761,000	$305,595
90			$10,579,000	$372,519
TOTAL	**$364,440**	**$728,880**	**$10,579,000**	**$8,509,966**

30 YEAR MORTGAGE PAYOFF *WITH* MPI™ FOCUS

AGE	MORTGAGE MONTHLY PAYMENT	MPI™ MONTHLY CONTRIBUTION	MPI™ ACCOUNT VALUE	ANNUAL RETIREMENT INCOME
30	$1,432	$1,605	$0	$0
35			$101,000	
40			$331,000	
45			$642,000	
50			$1,056,000	
55			$2,304,000	
60	$0	$0	$3,560,000	$391,600
70			$4,350,000	$467,998
80			$6,173,000	$570,487
90			$13,662,000	$695,421
TOTAL	**$515,609**	**$577,753**	**$13,662,000**	**$15,886,460**

*Assumed 60 Year Old Retirement Age. *Same Total Out of Pocket For Individual of $1,093,362 Over 30 Years. *4% Mortgage Interest Rate. *MPI™ Results Calculated From 2005-2019 S&P 500 Returns Repeated with COI For a 30-Year-Old Male, Preferred Health Rating. *Income Tax-Free Distributions. *Annual Income Increased 2% Per Year For Inflation. *MPI™ Account Value Equivalent to Cash Value Less Surrender Charges. *0% Floor, 11% Cap Used to Calculate Returns.

In the first scenario, the home-owner began "paying himself first" during years 11–30 for a total amount of $728,880. This produced more than $8,500,000 of retirement income and an inheritance of more than $10,500,000 by age 90. This is impressive and illustrates the power of compounding. $728,880 compounded through multiple cycles can produce up to $19,000,000 in wealth in 50 years. This is a great decision, but is it the best decision for YOUR money?

The second scenario makes "Pay Yourself First" a priority in your life, produces over $15,800,000 in retirement income and an inheritance of over $13,600,000. This results from contributing only $577,753 into MPI™, and allowing that contribution to compound for 60 years. More than $29,000,000 of compounding wealth produced with less money but requiring more time. More than $150,000 in interest was paid to the mortgage company (your cost) in exchange for roughly $10,000,000 (your benefit) more compounding wealth!

MPI™ > Accelerated Mortgage Pay Off

Recently, a system called Velocity Banking, has emerged as an amazing method to pay off your mortgage in 7 years. This sales system states you can pay off your mortgage through using a line of credit to accelerate the pay off. By using a line of credit, one would pay simple interest instead of amortized interest. Amortized interest is loaded heavier in the early years and tapers off where simple interest is a consistent value with lower payment early on.

It sounds amazing to have no mortgage in 7 years, however, it is the opposite of the maximization of Compound Interest in your life and mathematically false. These sales systems make outrageous claims that you "don't change your lifestyle" and "no change to your budget" which is not only misleading, but a blatant lie.

Here is an illustration representing a 35-year-old with a $300,000 mortgage comparing the Velocity Banking method to the 30-year amortized mortgage plus MPI™ Compounding (contributing only for the 7 years). In order to pay off a house in 7 years, the following is an example of what is would take, even assuming the line of credit was at 0%, 100% free money. Lines of credit are not 0%, but I want to give every possible advantage to illustrate how ridiculous the claim is that "you don't have to change your lifestyle" to have a mortgage paid off it 7 years.

VELOCITY BANKING- $300,000 MORTGAGE PAY OFF

AGE	MONTHLY VELOCITY PAYMENT	MPI™ MONTHLY CONTRIBUTION	MPI™ ACCOUNT VALUE	ANNUAL RETIREMENT INCOME
35	$3,571	$0	$0	$0
37				
39				
41				
50	PAID OFF			
55				
60				
65				
75	PAID OFF	-	-	-
85				
TOTAL	**$300,000**	**$0**	**$0**	**$0**

MPI™ FOCUS- $300,000 MORTGAGE PAY OFF

AGE	MONTHLY MORTGAGE PAYMENT	MPI™ MONTHLY CONTRIBUTION	MPI™ ACCOUNT VALUE	ANNUAL RETIREMENT INCOME
35			$24,600	
37	$1,432	$2,139	$77,400	
39			$136,500	
41			$213,700	-
50	$1,432 (PAID THROUGH LEVERAGE)	$0	$420,400	
55			$841,800	
60			$1,615,600	
65			$2,587,600	$309,000
75	PAID OFF	-	$3,346,500	$377,000
85			$6,496,000	$459,000
TOTAL	**$515,520**	**$179,676**	**$6,496,000**	**$7,979,000**

*Estimated Costs Taken From a 2019 NAIC Approved Illustration for a 35-Year-Old Male Preferred Health Rating. *Based on a 6.8% Annual Returns. *Assumed 4% Loan Rate for the MPI™ Secure Leverage Feature. *Annual Income Increased for Inflation. *Assumed 4% Interest Loan Rate.

A monthly mortgage of $1,432 to $3,571... That sounds like a little more than "no change in lifestyle" or budget. Velocity Banking assumes you have an extra $2,139 a month of disposable income you can use to pay off your mortgage. However, by making your regular mortgage payment of $1,432 and putting the extra $2,139 a month into a Secure Compounding

Account, you can pay your mortgage through your MPI™ account (The Pure Compounder—no additional money out of pocket), and have up to $2,500,000 by age 65 and a retirement income up to $310,000 annually. By age 85, you would have access to up to $7,900,000 in retirement income and cash value up to $6,500,000 because of a compounding decision made 50 years previous. Same amount of money, same amount of time; the difference is that one method focused on saving interest and the other focused on compounding interest!

The more irrational part of this sales pitch is that they then claim this is a great decision because you will have equity in your home you can use to invest! Starting your compound account is 7 years delayed.

Velocity is a really cool word but has zero mathematical validity. Math never lies!

MPI™ > Velocity Banking

The following page illustrates another scenario. This time, you receive an inheritance (or bonus or lottery win) of $300,000 and want to pay off your mortgage rather than allowing that lump sum to compound. How will this compare versus allowing the sum to compound inside of MPI™?

As a Pure Compounder, let's use of the leverage feature (a line of credit against your cash value) to pay the monthly mortgage, eliminating the mortgage payment from your cash flow, while allowing your inheritance to compound.

CHAPTER 10   MPI™ TO THE TEST   153

LUMP SUM MORTGAGE PAYOFF **WITH** MPI™ FOCUS

AGE	MORTGAGE MONTHLY PAYMENT	MPI™ MONTHLY CONTRIBUTION	MPI™ ACCOUNT VALUE	ANNUAL RETIREMENT INCOME
30	$0	$1,432	$0	$0
35			$90,000	
40			$295,000	
45			$573,000	
50			$942,000	
55			$2,056,000	
60	$0	$0	$3,176,000	$349,360
70			$3,881,000	$417,518
80			$6,125,000	$508,952
90			$12,118,900	$620,409
TOTAL	$0	$515,609	$12,118,900	$14,172,864

LUMP SUM MPI™ FOCUS _WITH_ 30 YEAR MORTGAGE PAYOFF

AGE	MORTGAGE MONTHLY PAYMENT	MPI™ LUMP SUM CONTRIBUTION	MPI™ ACCOUNT VALUE	ANNUAL RETIREMENT INCOME
30	$1,432 (PAID THROUGH LEVERAGE)	$300,000	$0	$0
35		-	$241,000	
40			$553,000	
45			$920,000	
50			$1,412,000	
55			$3,458,000	
60	$0	-	$5,410,000	$595,100
70			$7,447,000	$711,200
80			$9,487,000	$866,948
90			$24,003,000	$1,056,805
TOTAL	$515,609	$300,000	$24,003,000	$24,142,864

*Example Purposes Only As Lump Sum Payments Have Special Requirements. *Assumed 60 Year Old Retirement Age. *No Money Out of Pocket For Mortgage Payment. *4% Mortgage Interest Rate. *MPI™ Results Calculated From 2005-2019 S&P 500 Returns Repeated with COI For a 30-Year-Old Male, Preferred Health Rating. *Income Tax-Free Distributions *Annual Income Increased 2% Per Year For Inflation

$26,000,000 in value or $48,000,000 in value through the benefits of the ABC of Wealth!

MPI™ > Windfall Mortgage Pay Off

STUDENT LOANS

We have a massive Student Loan Crisis! Or do we? Not when we understand compounding using the ABC of Wealth! In the US, those with student debt carry an average of $35,000 at an average rate of 5.8%. The two scenarios are: 1) paying the loan in 10 years, then contributing the same payment amount for another 20 years thereafter; and 2) paying the minimum student loan payment for 30 years and compounding the "extra" that was being applied to student loan payments into MPI™ instead.

25-YEAR-OLD 10 YEAR STUDENT LOAN PAYOFF *THEN* MPI™ FOCUS

AGE	STUDENT LOAN MONTHLY PAY	MPI™ MONTHLY CONTRIBUTION	MPI™ ACCOUNT VALUE	ANNUAL RETIREMENT INCOME
25	$385	$0	-	$0
30				
35	$0	$385	$0	
40			$23,000	
45			$78,000	
50			$148,000	
55	$0	$0	$241,000	$26,510
65			$365,000	$31,682
75			$657,000	$38,620
85			$1,341,000	$47,078
TOTAL	$46,200	$92,400	$1,341,000	$1,075,460

25-YEAR-OLD 30 YEAR STUDENT LOAN PAYOFF *WITH* MPI™ FOCUS

AGE	STUDENT LOAN MONTHLY PAY	MPI™ MONTHLY CONTRIBUTION	MPI™ ACCOUNT VALUE	ANNUAL RETIREMENT INCOME
25			$0	$0
30			$11,000	
35	$206	$179	$36,000	
40			$71,000	
45			$117,000	
50			$257,000	
55	$0	$0	$397,000	$43,670
65			$485,000	$52,190
75			$688,000	$63,619
85			$1,523,000	$77,551
TOTAL	$74,160	$64,440	$1,523,000	$1,771,608

*Assumed 55 Year Old Retirement Age. *Same Total Out of Pocket For Individual Over 30 Years. *5.8% Student Loan Interest Rate. *MPI™ Results Calculated From 2005-2019 S&P 500 Returns Repeated with COI For a 25-Year-Old Male, Preferred Health Rating. *Income Tax-Free Distributions. *Annual Income Increased 2% Per Year For Inflation. *v Equivalent to Cash Value Less Surrender Charges. *0% Floor, 11% Cap Used to Calculate Returns.

By paying yourself first in MPI™ as soon as possible, focusing on compounding provided a path to as much as 65% more retirement income.

In similar fashion as the lump mortgage payoff scenarios, the paying off debt sooner or with a lump sum, impedes the benefits of compounding because of time. Time gives you one, two, three, or more additional Compound Cycles (depending on how soon you Pay Yourself First).

This is exactly the opposite of what we've been taught in school or led to believe by "experts." By paying the minimum required amount to simple interest and empowering your money to begin compounding immediately, you've just started your future self on the road to sustained wealth.

MPI™ > Student Loan Debt Pay Off

529 CHILD EDUCATION SAVINGS PLAN

The 529 Child Education Plan is a tax-advantaged savings vehicle that can be used for qualified education expenses. This heavily promoted mainstream investment concept follows the same linear mindset as what we accept as those "best" solutions recommended for retirement planning in our 401(k) and IRA. If started when a child is born, you can contribute for about 18 years until the beneficiary enters college, invested with a menu of typical mutual fund options comprised of stocks/bonds. Just like retirement accounts, we get out of the gate sprinting with an aggressive portfolio and arrive freshman year of college "walking" with a conservative portfolio.

This scenario is just as backward as our 401(k) and IRAs. However, the 529 plan goes one step further, making it what I consider the worst compounding account ever designed.

Why?

The 529 is not only built as a risk-based model that slows down over time, but the financial world believes and promotes killing the compounding effects inside this account. You potentially have 18 years to build an account that achieves up to three Compound Cycles, ready to truly reap the reward for your discipline and time in compounding, only to throw it all away for the "feel good" of saving some "linear thinking" simple interest.

Let's examine how devastating the math truly is: Consider a parent who saves $250/month when a child is born until they are 18. What happens from that point on?

Let's compare the 529 plan with an MPI™ college savings plan and observe the difference in their outcomes. Like the other example, we will use the leverage feature to pay all payments for the debt incurred by the student to attend college and pay it off as slowly as possible.

The results are an accurate example of what has happened in the market over the last 15 years. The power of compounding plus time is real. Killing a compounding account at 18 years old will cost you, or your child, a "near guaranteed" future full of prosperity and abundance all for the linear driven notion that debt (using someone else's money) is a like cancer and should be avoided at all cost.

529 DEBT-FREE FOCUS

YEAR	529 MONTHLY CONTRIBUTION	529 ACCOUNT VALUE	STUDENT DEBT	MONTHLY INTEREST PAYMENTS
1	$250	$0	$0	$0
6		$21,000		
12		$63,000		
18		$137,000		
24	-	$0	$0	$0

MPI™ COMPOUND FOCUS

YEAR	MPI™ MONTHLY CONTRIBUTION	MPI™ ACCOUNT VALUE	STUDENT LOAN BALANCE	MONTHLY INTEREST PAYMENTS
1	$250	$0	$0	$0
6		$21,000		
12		$63,000		
18		$137,000		
24		$266,000	$137,000	
30		$433,000	$124,000	
36	-	$694,000	$107,000	$804 (PAID THROUGH LEVERAGE)
42		$1,195,000	$82,000	
48		$1,916,000	$48,000	
54	-	$3,305,000	$0	$0
RETIREMENT INCOME @ 54 YEARS OLD		**$363,550 TAX-FREE ANNUALLY**		

*Total Out-of-Pocket For Parents is $54,000. *No Additional Contributions After 18 Years. *MPI™ Results Calculated From 2005-2019 S&P 500 Returns Repeated with COI For a Newborn. *5.8% Student Loan Interest Rate. *0% Floor, 11% Cap Used to Calculate Returns. *4% Loan Rate on Leveraged Money From MPI™.

By age 54, there is the potential to accumulate $3,300,000 in this account **after** paying 100% of all student loan payments from this same account. Your child could leave college having had no out-of-pocket expenses AND through the power of compounding and the ABC of Wealth, end up a millionaire. Starting an MPI™ account for a child is possibly the greatest blessing you could do for their long-term financial security: they end up college-educated, debt free, and have a secure financial future.

Is it a *good* idea for your child to leave college debt-free? Of course! ***Unless*** it is to the detriment of compounding. Although it sounds good to leave college debt-free, the ABC of Wealth shows you the best path, because with money, compounding with TIME always wins!

MPI™ > 529 Plan

RENT VS BUY

Should you rent or buy a house? This decision is one of the few where the answer is: "it depends." Individual situations and goals determine if renting is "throwing money away" or if buying a house is a sound financial decision.

Ownership includes expenses such as taxes, insurance, maintenance, and remodeling every 15–25 years. An owner can expect appreciation, generally equal to that of the inflation rate, over the long-term.

That said, the math shows that buying a house is not a great investment. However, buying a house provides structure and security to raise a family. This is one of the "feel goods" that might make sense for those who value a specific environment for a family.

Like many, we bought our house (with a mortgage) because we enjoy the freedom of choice that comes from ownership, from painting walls to landscaping the yard. It also establishes permanence for the kids as they remain in the same school system for as long as we choose.

Now, how do we apply the ABC of Wealth to the scenario of rent vs own? Is ownership limited by having the amount for a down payment? Are there any clear scenarios that are good, better, and best.

If no down payment were required to buy a house, then buying or renting would have a very similar financial impact on your life. Neither is a great investment but buying does offer the structure and flexibility for a family, with some additional benefits of asset-appreciation.

However, let's look at how a 20% down payment requirement changes your wealth.

HOME PURCHASE *WITH* 20% DOWN PAYMENT

AGE	MONTHLY MORTGAGE PAYMENT	DOWN PAYMENT	HOME VALUE	ANNUAL RETIREMENT INCOME
30	$1,145 (PLUS TAXES, INSURANCE, MAINTENANCE)	$60,000	$300,000	$0
35			$364,000	
40			$444,000	
45		-	$540,000	
50			$657,000	
55			$799,000	
60			$973,000	
70	PAID OFF	-	$1,183,000	NO MORTGAGE (STILL OWE TAXES, INSURANCE, ETC.)
80			$1,440,000	
90			$1,752,000	
TOTAL	$412,487	$60,000	$1,752,000	$0

RENTING *WITH* MPI™ FOCUS

AGE	MONTHLY RENTAL PAYMENT	MPI™ CONTRIBUTION	MPI™ ACCOUNT VALUE	ANNUAL RETIREMENT INCOME
30	$1,800	$60,000	$0	$0
35	$2,087		$66,000	
40	$2,419		$151,000	
45	$2,804	-	$252,000	
50	$3,251		$384,000	
55	$3,769		$833,000	
60	$4,369		$1,273,000	$140,030
70	$5,872	-	$1,664,000	$167,349
80	$7,891		$3,133,000	$203,997
90	$10,605		$6,116,000	$248,672
TOTAL	$3,649,213	$60,000	$6,116,000	$5,680,748

*Example Purposes Only as Lump Sum Contribution has Special Requirements. *Assumed 60 Year Old Retirement Age. *Taxes, Insurance, and Maintenance Projected at 50% of Mortgage or $600/Month. *4% Mortgage Interest Rate. *MPI™ Results Calculated From 2005-2019 S&P 500 Returns Repeated with COI For a 30-Year-Old Male, Preferred Health Rating.*Income Tax-Free Distributions. *Annual Income Increased 2% Per Year For Inflation. *0% Floor, 11% Cap Used to Calculate Returns.

Owning a home worth close to $1,000,000 outright when you hit retirement age sounds nice. It is not a bad situation to be in. You would have no mortgage payment, but would still be responsible for expenses like taxes, insurance, maintenance, etc. But how much retirement income does this home produce for you?

ZERO!

However, how much impact does the $60,000 down payment have for you and your financial freedom? By the time you would have paid off your mortgage with a $1,000,000 in real-estate equity, that $60,000 inside of MPI™ would have created value totaling around $1,200,000 of liquid wealth capable of producing long-term income for you. You could expect around a $140,000 tax-free annual income for life from MPI™.

That $60,000 "down payment" would produce around $11,700,000 in value to your life over a compounding span of 60 years. A paid-off house, which produces zero retirement income, would bring a value of around $1,700,000 over the same 60 years.

But as mentioned, I bought my house with a $60,000 down payment. How did I do that? Through the ABC of Wealth. By paying myself first, contributing extra money to my MPI™ account and achieving "Pure Compounder" status quickly, I had additional leveragability in my account. In the same scenario, but waiting a few extra years to buy the house, and then using the Participating Loan to leverage the down payment, what would the potential outcome be?

At year 7, one could borrow $60,000 from the account. What is the impact to our MPI™ scenario by doing this? Rather than $1,200,000 in account value in 30 years, the account would have around $1,000,000 capable of producing a retirement income of around $110,000. You can enjoy the best of both worlds when you apply a little time, discipline, and patience to your money.

MPI™ > Renting or Buying

SINGLE FAMILY RENTALS

There may be no other concept more readily accepted as "secure retirement income" stemming from owning a single-family rental. What if I told you this one strategy is little more than a linear function, preventing your money from producing wealth? Single family rentals not only require a lot of work, they also present the risk of property damage, evictions, and other liabilities.

They simply do not compound and will nearly always underperform given other options your money has to work for you. For example, I have an aunt with a $400,000 balance in her 401(k). Her retirement strategy is to buy two rental properties outright with her 401(k) savings, expecting to produce around $2,000 of net income (after expenses) per month adding to what she will receive from Social Security. This is a pretty good plan. Let's compare it to using the ABC of Wealth through MPI™:

PURCHASING 2 SINGLE FAMILY RENTALS

AGE	MONTHLY MORTGAGE	PURCHASE PRICE	EQUITY VALUE (2 HOUSES)	RENTAL INCOME (AFTER TAXES, INSURANCE, ETC)
65		$400,000	$400,000	$24,000
70			$486,000	$27,823
75	PAID OFF		$592,000	$32,254
80		-	$720,000	$37,391
85			$876,000	$43,347
90			$1,066,000	$50,251
TOTAL	-	$400,000	$1,066,000	$925,273

MPI™ LEGACY PLAN

AGE	MPI™ LUMP SUM CONTRIBUTION	MPI™ ACCOUNT VALUE	TOTAL LEGACY BENEFIT	RETIREMENT INCOME
65	$400,000	-	$6,300,000	$44,000
70		$281,000	$6,418,000	$47,627
75		$345,000	$6,500,000	$52,584
80		$687,000	$6,800,000	$58,058
85		$1,600,000	$7,800,000	$64,100
90		$2,900,000	$9,100,000	$70,771
TOTAL	$400,000	$2,900,000	$9,100,000	$1,409,333

*Example Purposes Only as Lump Sum Contribution has Special Requirements. *MPI™ Legacy Plan Is an Exclusive Plan For Retirees and Has Special Requirements. ¹Assumed 65 Year Old Retirement Age. ²Taxes, Insurance, and Maintenance Projected at 33% of Rent. ³MPI™ Results Calculated From 2005-2019 S&P 500 Returns Repeated. ⁴Income Tax-Free Distributions. ⁵Annual Income Increased 2% Per Year For

As you can see, a $400,000 investment into two rentals produced around $1,000,000 of retirement income over 25 years and around $1,000,000 in inheritance to leave to beneficiaries. This sounds good. However, through the secure compounding of MPI™, a significant increase in income can occur; furthermore, MPI™ can generate a total value to the family/estate of around $10,500,000 when including the life insurance and other benefits.

In this graphic, I mentioned the MPI™ Legacy Plan, which is a specifically designed plan for people who have either health concerns or are too old to qualify for the MPI™ Plan. For more information regarding the Legacy Plan, please reach out and we can customize a plan for your situation.

MPI™ > Single Family Rentals

LEVERAGED REAL ESTATE

Real estate has one big advantage over most other investments; it routinely uses O.P.M. How does leveraged real estate compare with MPI™?

If there is any investment out there that can compete with MPI™, it should be a real estate portfolio, given that both use leverage. When designing MPI™, I followed the blueprint provided by real estate regarding the use of leverage. Without the role-model of real estate's innovative use of O.P.M., MPI™ might not exist today. MPI™ provides a path to leverage without the traditional risk of down markets, like the one we experienced in 2008, which left many real-estate investors in dire straits.

$200,000 LEVERAGED PURCHASING 5 SINGLE FAMILY RENTALS

AGE	DOWN PAYMENT (PER HOUSE X 5)	MONTHLY RENTAL INCOME (PER HOUSE X 5)	MONTHLY MORTGAGE (PER HOUSE X 5)	MONTHLY CASH FLOW AFTER MORTGAGE (PER HOUSE X 5)	EQUITY VALUE (PER HOUSE X 5)
30	$40,000	$1,000 (AFTER TAXES, INSURANCE, ETC)		$236	$200,000
35		$1,125		$361	$233,000
40		$1,300		$536	$284,000
45	$0	$1,512	$764	$748	$346,000
50		$1,750		$986	$421,000
55		$2,032		$1,268	$512,000
60		$2,356		$1,592	$623,000
70		$3,167		$3,167	$923,000
80		$4,256		$4,256	$1,366,000
90		$5720		$5,720	$2,023,000
TOTAL	$200,000 (ALL 5)	$9,783,180 (ALL 5)	$1,375,200 (ALL 5)	$8,407,980 (ALL 5)	$10,115,000 (ALL 5)

*4% Assumed Annual Increase in Equity Value. *3% Increase in Rental Income. *4% Loan Rate Used to Determine Monthly Mortgage.

A leveraged real estate plan beginning with a $200,000 investment for a 60-year period (including the owners required work managing these properties) produced very good results. It generated up to $8,000,000 in Cash Flow and $10,000,000 in Equity. Leverage is a powerful tool and can speed up all returns.

How can it produce these results? Because, for the most part, it follows $y = a(1 + r)^x$!

Did you invest into it? Yes. Immediately? Yes. Are rentals secure? Pretty secure. Do they grow in value? Yes. Did you leverage it to accelerate your growth potential? Yes.

Therefore, leveraged real estate rentals are an investment that follows the wealth equation. And if you can leverage real estate without a down payment requirement, that is a solid path to success.

Now, let's take the cash flow and compound it inside of MPI™ and compare it to taking the original $200,000 and immediately compounding it. What are the results?

REAL ESTATE CASH FLOW *WITH* MPI™ FOCUS

AGE	ANNUAL MPI™ CONTRIBUTION	MPI™ ACCOUNT VALUE	DEATH BENEFIT PAYOUT VALUE	ANNUAL RETIREMENT INCOME
30	$14,160	$0	$620,000	
35	$21,660	$93,000	$2,200,000	
40	$32,160	$341,000	$4,400,000	-
45	$44,880	$728,000	$5,800,000	
50	$59,160	$1,300,000	$6,300,000	
55	$76,080	$2,600,000	$7,700,000	
60	$95,520	$4,100,000	$9,200,000	$451,000
70	$190,020	$5,300,000	$10,400,000	$538,987
80	$255,360	$6,700,,000	$11,800,000	$657,022
90	$343,200	$9,900,000	$15,000,000	$800,806
TOTAL	$8,408,005	$9,900,000	$15,000,000	$18,296,204

$200,000 *WITH* MPI™ FOCUS

AGE	ANNUAL MPI™ CONTRIBUTION	MPI™ ACCOUNT VALUE	DEATH BENEFIT PAYOUT VALUE	ANNUAL RETIREMENT INCOME
30	$200,000	$0	$4,200,000	
35		$224,000	$4,424,000	
40		$553,000	$6,663,000	
45	$0	$965,000	$8,075,000	-
50		$1,542,000	$8,562,000	
55		$3,900,000	$11,000,000	
60		$6,300,000	$13,400,000	$693,000
70	$0	$9,500,000	$16,600,000	$828,199
80		$12,100,000	$19,200,000	$1,009,570
90		$33,000,000	$40,100,000	$1,230,660
TOTAL	$200,000	$33,000,000	$40,100,000	$28,113,679

*Example Purposes Only as Lump Sum Payment has Special Requirements. *Assumed 60 Year Old Retirement Age. *MPI™ Results Calculated From 2005-2019 S&P500 Returns Repeated. *Income Tax-Free Distributions. *Annual Income Increased 2% Per Year For Inflation. *0% Floor, 11% Cap Used to Calculate Returns.

A quick recap of the three scenarios

LEVERAGED REAL ESTATE/MPI™ SUMMARY

	LEVERAGED REAL ESTATE ONLY	LEVERAGED REAL ESTATE FUNDING MPI™	MPI™ ONLY
OUT OF POCKET	$200,000	$200,000	$200,000
EQUITY AFTER 60 YEARS (5 HOUSES)	$10,115,000	$10,115,000	$0
RETIREMENT INCOME	$8,408,005	$18,296,204	$28,113,679
ACCOUNT VALUE @90 YEARS OLD	EQUITY	$9,900,000	$33,000,000
INHERITANCE @90 YEARS OLD	$10,115,000	$15,000,000	$40,100,000
TOTAL VALUE RECEIVED	$18,523,005	$43,411,204	$68,213,679

*For Projected Returns, See Data Above in Previous Graphics.

When I first began this comparison, it surprised me that real estate did so well. This is another tribute to how true wealth can be achieved only through understanding the power of Secure Leverage.

All three of these scenarios are mind blowing. A $200,000 investment into real estate over 60 years can produce a value over $18,000,000 for you and your family. If you can continue to leverage and build your empire, you can increase it. You will end up rich given this scenario. It will require a lot of work, but this model is a solid business plan.

However, a leveraged real estate portfolio that uses cash flow to fund an MPI™ compounding account can produce up to $43,000,000 in total value. Why? Because the cash flow is being magnified by the compounding effects of your money. Once the compounding effects kick in, the difference is remarkable.

However, as with everything, there is good, better, and best. What is "best" in this example? Allowing compounding to occur as soon as possible, with as much as possible. We are good; compounding is better. By allowing compounding to do all the heavy lifting, it has the potential to produce up to $68,000,000 in your lifetime ($200,000 and a little over eight Compound Cycles in 60 years).

There is one big difference between these options. Two of the options require 60 years of property management, risk of property damage, evictions, maintenance, upgrades, and the various other headaches that come with owning real estate rentals. The third option was to Pay Yourself

First, today, somewhere secure, somewhere compounding, somewhere leverageable and get out of the way. That last option required no additional effort on your part aside from patience.

I can see why leveraged real estate is so attractive. Put those results against a traditional index fund and it would beat it up. But through the evolution of Secure Leverage, the ABC of Wealth will consistently provide the best path of wealth and security.

MPI™ > Leveraged Real Estate

ALL IN ONE BUSINESS

I am pro-business. I love everything about start-up. I embrace the struggles and stresses that are required in this world. Few people are built to handle the true nature of business and all the responsibilities and obligations that come with it. I also believe the entrepreneurial spirit is what makes America great. We all want the best, and many people are willing to go get it. And if "best" doesn't exist, then they innovate and make it!

There is a common theme in the entrepreneurial world that a small-business owner should always go ALL-IN on their business. This includes 100% of their life savings, 16-hour workdays, borrowing money from friends and family, sacrificing time with their family, and various other extremes that may be needed to chase "the dream."

I believe and support most of this but with one twist. Because the majority of businesses don't survive longer than 20 years, I have one important message for all entrepreneurs!

You are in business for one main objective: to protect and secure your future self!!!

Yes, we want to bring value to the world, help others, and a variety of other good causes, but if your #1 goal is not to protect your future self and your long-term security and freedom, you will not be able to offer the most value to the world, to help the most amount of people, or achieve the freedom you seek.

As I write this book, nearly every small business has been forced to close their doors due to the COVID-19 pandemic of 2020. This course of action has never occurred in my lifetime, nor in the lifetime of anyone I know. A new precedent has been set that your business will never be safe again from these types of reactions or mandated expectations.

For this reason, I heavily promote a unique concept. Rather than taking your "profits" and reinvesting back into the business, as is often suggested, I have a different approach. Can you guess what it is? Pay Yourself First!

A full 50% of all your NET profits should be going to yourself first. You earned it. You deserve it. The next 50% then goes to your business expansion

If you are willing to make this decision, that your future self comes first, the protection of your family and business have top priority over sprinting and "scaling" as fast as possible, you will find yourself with more confidence, security, and as time goes on, an increase in total wealth.

For example, let's say your business made $50,000 NET profit and you decided to make security and compounding the focus. By taking $25,000 a year and starting an MPI™ Business Protection Plan, over the next 20 years, you could provide your business with the following protection: The majority (outside of Surrender Charge) of this account value would be liquid and available to you for emergencies, weathering the storm of a COVID-19 future scenario, or could be added to your current retirement plan.

MPI™ BUSINESS PROTECTION PLAN

YEAR	ANNUAL CONTRIBUTION	MPI™ ACCOUNT VALUE
5	$25,000	$133,000
10	$25,000	$354,000
15	$25,000	$743,000
20	$25,000	$1,408,000

*Estimated Costs Taken From a 2019 NAIC Approved Illustration for a 35-Year-Old Male Preferred Health Rating. *Based on a 6.8% Annual Returns. *Assumed 4% Loan Rate for the MPI™ Secure Leverage Feature.

As you can see, by saving 50% of your profits, your MPI™ Account would grow very quickly, producing immeasurable security and confidence for your future. At year 10, when you need funds to buy some additional machinery, or survive a down market, or additional liquidity to meet payroll, you would have it available.

Why do I believe in this message so much?

From 2004–2014, I ran a successful granite countertop business. The business was making high 6-figures, even surpassing 7-figures in 2013, I paid myself a modest salary of $120,000 annually running a $10,000,000 business while investing all the profits back into the business. I paid for machinery with cash, had no debt, paid for all my inventory, and expanded the business at a rapid pace. I had a net worth of millions of dollars, but there is one thing I didn't have, which is where most businesses fail. I didn't have liquidity.

Over a 6-month span in 2014, due to some extreme, unforeseen circumstances, because all my assets were tied up, not liquid, or in Accounts Receivables, and still had all the liabilities of overhead, payroll, etc., the business was forced to shut down. I couldn't weather the storm. 10 years of my career lost in a short amount of time because I didn't plan for a rainy day. We never think it is going to rain and when it starts, it is too late. I had millions of dollars in value, equity, inventory, machinery, but no accessibility to immediate security. This is a common theme and reason small businesses are forced to close their doors every day.

Six years ago, I started my own MPI™ Business Protection Plan. It was the single best business decision I've ever made. Why? Because right now I have sufficient reserves in my MPI™ Plan to sleep with confidence. I have no worries about my business right now, and I also have liquidity to continue to expand my business and maintain my projected business growth. I take 50% (minimum) of all my net profits and put it securely toward compounding for my future.

 This value is beyond measure. For six years I had been told I was doing it wrong, even ridiculed for not capitalizing on the "bull market." I was told by investing gurus I could use my profits to "expand" faster and to "invest" more aggressively. But that is not how long-term sustainability can be achieved. The foundation of security and compounding must go out before it goes up. I built my foundation and now can survive the Armageddon to small businesses, the unthinkable scenario of the government forcing my business to close.

You are in business to protect yourself, your family, your employees, and their families. By taking 50% of your NET profits (or anything you can) and starting it compounding for a rainy day today, you will look back at that decision and understand why it was one of the best decisions of your life. Confidence, security, and freedom—that is what Secure Compounding can provide your life!

MPI™ > The Unknown Future

STARTING NOW or LATER

How powerful is starting today? I often see influencers on Social Media post memes saying, "What are the most important actions to take in your 20s?" These memes always list the same things: Read books, get a mentor, go to conventions, start a side hustle, go to school, get out of debt, and many other good suggestions, but I have yet to see even one financial influencer tell a 20-year-old to start a compounding account as soon as they begin their first job, graduate from high school, or get out of college. It seems kind of crazy to me that this is not #1 on every list, as it is a near guaranteed path to becoming a millionaire. Because basic mathematics are not universally understood, more "feel good" advice is given due to the notion that young people "have plenty of time." But does anyone really have time to wait? Compound Interest waits for no one!

Let me illustrate what I mean by comparing Compound Cycles relative to a newborn, a 25-year-old and a 45-year-old. If $250 per month were set aside for 20 years for each of these individuals, after which, deposits cease allowing it to compound on its own, what kind of compounding is achieved when they are each 65 years old? Each scenario has a total contribution of $60,000. Now let's see how each one responds to the effect of time:

$250 MONTHLY CONTRIBUTION TO MPI™ FOR 20 YEARS			
	NEWBORN	25-YEAR-OLD	45-YEAR-OLD
MONTHLY CONTRIBUTION	$250	$250	$250
TOTAL CONTRIBUTION	$60,000	$60,000	$60,000
ACCOUNT VALUE @65 YEARS OLD	$3,600,000	$1,000,000	$175,000
RETIREMENT INCOME @65 YEARS OLD	$396,000	$110,000	$19,250
COST PER DAY DELAYING YOUR MPI™ PLAN	$1,084	$301	$52

*Assumed 65 Year Old Retirement Age. *MPI™ Results Calculated From 2005-2019 S&P 500 Returns Repeated with COI For the Respective Ages Listed Above. *Income Tax-Free Distributions. *0% Floor, 11% Cap Used to Calculate Returns. *Assumed Funding For 20 Years Only.

The power of time and compounding. The same amount of invested money compounding but with varying timelines. The cost of delaying compounding is immeasurable when one considers the freedom money can provide.

What is the income potential at age 65 for the newborn, the 25-year-old, and the 45-year-old who began compounding at the same time? Look at the amount of money it is costing PER DAY to take advantage of compounding!

Compound Interest has the potential to make hundreds of thousands per year in retirement income. Divide the annual retirement income potential by 365 days to see what it is costing per day to delay. Rule #2, "Start Today," is not only a motivational tool. It will potentially make thousands of dollars a day for your future self.

Finally, there is one last concept to reinforce regarding the theory of Compound Cycles and Time. Though you have much to consider already, along with all the previous illustrations, this will be the most powerful point of all. Because a Compound Cycle is the doubling of your money, your investment in the first cycle will have more influence than all other contributions thereafter! This concept is so powerful that the moment I understood it, it became the driving force to compound as much money as possible, without delay, in my own plan!

The power of the first cycle, the spark for the engine to run, is the source of unlimited wealth. Because money is doubling, the first eight years of contributions (assuming a seven-year Compound Cycle) will produce more Compound Interest than all other future-year investments combined, no matter how long you invest after the 8th year.

You can invest from years 8–100, 8–1000, 8–1,000,000, and it will never catch up to the first eight years of compounding. Not a penny more! Obviously more money in the first cycle only makes the results better.

How can this be?

The power lies in the Compound Cycle, the doubling of your money! Starting immediately and making compounding an integral part of your life will not only benefit you, but your children, their children, and generations to come.

	START NOW		START IN 8 YEARS	
YEAR	INVESTMENT	ACCOUNT VALUE	INVESTMENT	ACCOUNT VALUE
1	$5,000	$5,517	-	-
2	$5,000	$11,603	-	-
3	$5,000	$18,318	-	-
4	$5,000	$25,727	-	-
5	$5,000	$33,901	-	-
6	$5,000	$42,919	-	-
7	$5,000	$52,869	-	-
8	$5,000	$63,847	$5,000	$5,517
9	-	$70,443	$5,000	$11,603
10	-	$77,719	$5,000	$18,318
11	-	$85,748	$5,000	$25,727
12	-	$94,605	$5,000	$33,901
13	-	$104,378	$5,000	$42,919
14	-	$115,160	$5,000	$52,869
15	-	$127,056	$5,000	$63,847
20	-	$207,714	$5,000	$138,279
30	-	$555,138	$5,000	$458,888
40	-	$1,483,669	$5,000	$1,315,753
50	-	$3,965,275	$5,000	$3,605,820
60	-	$10,597,648	$5,000	$9,726,287
70	-	$28,323,419	$5,000	$26,083,929
80	-	$75,697,557	$5,000	$69,801,586
90	-	$202,310,323	$5,000	$186,641,994
100	-	$540,697,331	$5,000	$498,911,262
TOTAL	$40,000	$540,697,331	$465,000	$498,911,262

*Projecting an Estimated 7 Year Compound Cycle.

A $5,000 investment for eight years into a newborn's MPI™ plan can produce up to $540,000,000 in their lifetime. Compound Interest! The 8th wonder of the world, the most powerful force in the Universe, and the greatest mathematical discovery of all time. I cannot overstate how much value this can bring to your life! But it all goes back to "He who understands it, earns it!" What will you do with this knowledge now?

> *"The Essence of Mathematics is
> not to Make Simple Things Complicated,
> but to Make Complicated Things Simple."*
>
> **S. Gudder**

NOTES/THOUGHTS

CHAPTER 11
Early Adopters

Consider the positives: Increased retirement income by up to 400%? Life insurance, Living Benefits, tax advantages, guaranteed security, and better results, all in the same system? O.P.M. advantages provided even to the everyday American, not just the wealthy? All backed and managed by a multi-billion-dollar, A+ Rated Life insurance company that has been in business for over 100 years?

Why does the notion that slow, steady, and secure, allowing Compound Interest to do all the heavy lifting over time, sound amazing to some, too good to be true to others, like a scam to competitors, and complete abstract craziness to the rest? Because of Biology! We are all wired differently.

In a well-known book called *Diffusions of Innovation* (1962), Everett Rogers, a professor of communications, explained "how, why, and at what rate new ideas and technology spread" or are accepted across the population. In society, our population is typically dispersed across five categories of acceptance.

1. Innovators. Comprised of around 2.5% of the population: people who introduce new methods, ideas, or products. This segment of society does not fear change, always asks "why" we do things the way we do them, and creates advances in technology, business, concepts, and the way we view the world. Most people reject innovators at first because they present ideas that seem "different," "unfamiliar," "too good to be true," or plain "crazy." This group created the airplane, car, TV, camera, streaming

services, smartphone, and all the innovations we take for granted now in society. Things happen because someone thought it was possible.

2. Early Adopters (First Followers). Represent around 13.5% of the population: people who "just get it"; they embrace evolution, truth, and innovation with ease. These people are "open" to new ideas, do their own research, reach their own conclusions, trust their gut, and confidently make decisions, even when they are contrary to what they previously were told or believed. They like to be on the forefront of new and improved methods of life and always strive for the best path. They bought a smartphone the moment they could and frequently "pre-purchase" the new model.

3. Early Majority. Consisting of about 34% of the population: people who like innovation but prefer not to be the first to challenge the status quo. These people benefit and await the validation stemming from the Early Adopters. Biology impedes them from the unfamiliar until they see others doing it. They typically do some basic research, enjoy what they are hearing and seeing, but wait until others confirm their opinions. After they had seen some examples of a smartphone, saw many using them, they jumped in the pool.

4. Late Majority. This is around 34% of the population: people who follow what everyone else is doing. They do not do their own research, are comfortable following the majority, and trust the opinion of the masses. They embrace the status quo even to their own detriment. Their smartphone is frequently an older model, but still a smartphone.

5. Laggards. They are about 16% of the population: people forced to join the rest because it is the only thing available. They stick with the old, comfortable, and familiar until it is no longer

available. They have a basic cell phone, won't text, don't care about innovations in smartphones and become irritated when forced to "upgrade away" from the obsolete.

Which are you? As individuals, we are not bound to one category for life.

I love the innovation process, have multiple patents in various industries, and feel I'm in the 2.5% of the population who is always questioning the why (of things I find intriguing) and seeking my best life. However, I was an Early Majority for the smartphone. I kept my Blackberry Pearl as long as I could. It functioned exactly the way I wanted, and I could text so quickly on it!

All five categories resonate in some part of my life because my energy flows in different ways throughout my life. For example, the other day, a new client committed to their MPI™ financial plan. I then drove it to the brokerage (45 mins away) because my wife was out of town. She is the one who scans and emails any contract. I've never scanned something before, so rather than learning or googling how to do it, I got in my car and drove. I'm a Laggard when it comes to scanning documents.

I share this to show my understanding of the emotions stirred by overturning the financial-planning apple cart. Some of you find it exciting to hear the power of Compound Interest and want to take advantage of it as soon as possible. You would call me right now if you had my number.

To some of you it sounds great, but a little scary. It is really this simple? Is there anyone who can validate it? Can you really achieve wealth in your life making $40,000 a year and just compounding some of it?

To some of you, this is total BS because your financial advisor (or maybe you are a financial advisor) would have told you about it already if it really worked like this.

And lastly, to some, you have no clue what I'm talking about. You will probably never read this because you didn't make it this far in the book. It is way too complex, so you will just continue with your 401(k) until your company provides something different.

None of these feelings are wrong, they are biology expressing why you feel the way you feel.

It is my strong desire and priority to share my well-researched knowledge on the Rules of Money, motivate you to learn the universal laws that govern Compound Interest, apply them to maximize their potential in your life, and understand the fundamental mathematics of Compound Cycles to achieve an unlimited amount of success in your life. This will be one of the most important things you could ever learn and will provide more freedom than anything else you put energy into. And the best part is that it is simple. After a few hours dedicated to the understanding of Compound Interest, you will know enough to get your money working for you for the rest of your life!

It took 6 years for MPI™ to be conceived, designed, tested, and ultimately built. From the beginning our goal has been to create more predictable and secure results, having drawn thousands of Early Adopters during the first two years of release.

At the MPI™ launch in 2018, people had never seen anything like it. My claim that it could increase retirement income by up to 400% over traditional investment solutions sounded ludicrous, given that some described me as this "dude in Gilbert, Arizona, designing a financial strategy, with no background in finances, that beat all the other gurus by significant amounts." But as time goes on, the Early Adopters have paved a way for rapid acceptance as they build the foundation to reap the rewards of secure compounding.

This book is my invitation to you to investigate what I'm saying, study it with your spouse and children (if you have a family), fact check anything I claim, do your own research (don't get deceived by linear minded people) and follow your heart as truth is truth. You need not feel scared as thousands have paved the way before you. If you feel MPI™ could be right for you, reach out to me TODAY. Do not delay! Let's build your plan now and start the path of becoming a Pure Compounder.

I am grateful for so many Early Adopters: individuals across the country who researched, validated, believed, and trust in the power of MPI™ to shape their future. These individuals push me to be better, always sharing their ideas, concerns, fears, and excitement, so I can provide the best education possible in sharing my message with the world. Some I have never met in person yet consider them both family and friends. How do they feel about MPI™? Here are their own words:

"Curtis is BRILLIANT! MPI™ was a tough sell for my wife and me. I am the son of a very successful financial planner and had been investing in a Roth IRA since the age of 16. I never really questioned the system because I trusted my dad's old school method of saving for retirement and had accumulated a good amount of money through the power of Compound Interest during the 18 years I devoted to my Roth. When Curtis explained the MPI™ system to my wife and me, we knew immediately he had created something special. It not only allows us to take advantage of the Compound Interest we had with the Roth IRA, but also leverage against ourselves with a secure 0% floor through a life insurance policy for the both of us! Our goal has always been to establish the best financial future for our family and MPI™ is the program that will achieve our retirement dreams."
—**Lance Watson, Scottsdale, Arizona**

"After my husband died at 57 from cancer leaving me to provide for two teenagers, a family member fortunately had an investment business and helped me roll over insurance and 401(k)'s into mutual funds. As time passed, I began to educate myself with other options about trusts, insurance, fixed annuities, and Compound Interest. When I heard Curtis Ray speak on his MPI™ system, the zero-floor protecting my principal plus the best of the other investment vehicles were what I had been seeking. Curtis' patience, integrity and heart shown through as he answered my questions. This will change my family tree forever."
—**Celia Hansell, Grand Saline, Texas**

"I never felt right about locking my money away in an IRA or a 401(k). I was hopeful that as an entrepreneur I could just create my retirement income with a couple rental properties and another business. Curtis is mindful, transparent and enthusiastic about people creating wealth. For me, the strategy he created explains how to actually utilize Compound Interest to its full potential, whereas others are just hoping. I 100% recommend the MPI™ system to families wanting to create amazing futures for themselves,

as well as being the reason that their kids and their kids will be wealthy for generations to come."
— **Matt Ogle, Boise, Idaho**

"I met Curtis at a mutual friend's birthday party, and we engaged in a casual conversation about investing. I could tell he truly believed he came up with the "Holy Grail" of investing so I made sure we got together again to discuss his program, MPI™. After a few meetings, I saw how powerful MPI™ was and could not stop thinking about it. Although I spent the next few months trying to find the hole in MPI™, I was unsuccessful. After months of research and validation, all I wanted to do was get my money into it as soon as possible and let it grow exponentially for me. I was always good at living within my means and saving up a few bucks, but I was torn on what to do with it. I was somewhere between investing in stocks on my own or real estate. Luckily, I met Curtis before I made any regrettable decisions with it. Now, I can focus on my job and sleep well knowing that my financial future is extremely bright! MPI™ will bring financial freedom to me much sooner and to a much higher degree than anything else that I could've invested in. I think Warren Buffet would be a huge fan of MPI™, after all he said "Rule No. 1: Never lose money. Rule No. 2: Never forget rule No. 1."
— **Adam Rummler, Phoenix, Arizona**

"We recognized immediately that the education Curtis Ray provided was not only different but special. The concepts, while simple, take on a very practical and sustainable method through its combination and execution. This is contrary to conventional thought yet resonates with truth and common sense. After meeting Curtis, it was evident that his passion is to empower others with this transformative information. We are fortunate that this brilliant man has the ability to present this information in a clear, concise, and straightforward manner. If you desire to have peace of mind preparing for retirement, you will benefit greatly from Curtis' teachings."
— **Tim Luke MD, Sonya Luke PharmD, Scottsdale, Arizona**

There are hundreds more who are willing and eager to share their experience with MPI™; their testimonials could comprise a book by itself. My offer of accountability and transparency is the result of being in the public eye these past two years following the launch of MPI™.

Because biology pre-disposes a large percentage of the population to be skeptical, questioning, and suspicious of the new and unfamiliar, much of my time has been spent validating my math.

As time goes on and to my surprise, I've come to realize that it's not just about the math. It's about the story, the evolution, connection, the answers to address fears and questions you might have. This, combined with MPI™ being backed by one of the most reputable insurance companies in the world, provide the security, confidence, and value to those who are seeking better for their financial future.

When you are ready to take this step into compounding your life, I can make two guarantees:

1. I will fully and completely answer any and all questions you have regarding this ground-breaking financial planning strategy, how it can serve your dreams, and provide you a clear path to success.
2. This is my own plan for my own future and protection of my family. I will do everything in my power to assure the security and success of MPI™. Because of the theory of "Pure Compounder," I contribute every dollar possible into my MPI™ plan. My money is my money to keep, creating compound growth that fuels my ability to spend freely and to openly provide value to others!

> *"The First Follower is Actually an Underestimated Form of Leadership in Itself . . . The First Follower is What Transforms a Lone Nut into a Leader."*
>
> **Derek Sivers**

NOTES/THOUGHTS

CHAPTER 12

Everyone Ends Up Rich

The year is 2050, the American economy is booming, the average household income is greater than $100,000 annually (in today's dollar value) and prosperity has been achieved by most Americans. Understanding how money works, and its simplicity, has become a focused part of society. "The ABC of Wealth" course is mandatory for high school graduation and is taught from elementary school through college. The fundamental principles of Compound Interest are available to everyone. Everyone Ends Up Rich™!

This is my vision for a world in which understanding Compound Interest is a priority. It is 2020 as I write this book; within the next 30 years, world hunger will cease to exist, clean water will be available to all, and prosperity in the world will reach the ends of the earth through the efforts of exponential thinking people! Sound like a fairytale? Sound too good to be true? Albert Einstein didn't think so . . . nor do I.

Compound Interest is an energy so powerful, it can fix any financial situation, no matter how severe. We have the roadmap showing us the way to wealth without failure, a method to climb out of any hole, and the solution to any problem placed in front of us, financial or otherwise.

I believe in the energy of money. I believe we have something life-changing at our disposal that was always there, right in front of us. We just couldn't see it because of all the noise produced by greed, hype, or plain ignorance due to what we were taught and continue to believe about money. However, the moment we understand and apply the wisdom, financial independence and freedom are the results, every single time. Always Be Compounding!

Can everyone really end up rich? The answer to that question is simple: YES! Think Compounding! ABC your life. That's the only requirement. We all possess the ability to bridge the gap in the mind from linear thinking to exponential acceptance, thereby making decisions that have compounding potential. Everyone can thrive in a system designed around living within the laws that govern Compound Interest. It is that simple. In this book, I hope you have learned exactly what Compound Interest is, as well as everything you need to know to maximize and optimize its power in your life today.

Will Everyone End Up Rich? That is an entirely different conversation in and of itself. The Linear Mindset is strong. It "feels" so good because we see results immediately. On the surface, linear solutions make sense with little to no explanation: Pay off your debt? OK! Defer your taxes? Of course! Home run potential? Yes, please! Cash Flow Real Estate? Bling Bling! Long-term, optimized, best results? Mathematically impossible!

As a society, we have neglected teaching this knowledge in business, school, church, community, or anywhere else. We don't even teach our kids about money saying insane things like "they need to find their own way" or "I don't want to ruin my kids." Why wouldn't we want our kids to have the freedom we never had, freedom based in learning about slow, steady, and secure compounding? When the influence/power of Compound Interest is explained, our natural reaction is "too good to be true." Our brains are wired this way. But those who understand that tomorrow's security supersedes today's satisfaction reap the rewards of unrestrained prosperity.

February 25th, 2019 was a significant event only a few select people in my life know about until now. Because I believe it is an important part of my story, I have decided to include it in this book. Some of you might think it is crazy, others may be supportive, but ultimately, it is part of who I am!

On the evening of February 23rd, 2019, a Saturday night, I was researching Einstein, Compound Interest, and the Rules of Wealth so I could better explain this amazing power to others. I focus most of my time on reading about finance and how I can better connect with people to motivate them towards educating themselves.

While I was researching, I came across a very disturbing article predicting the collapse of the US monetary system as we know it, giving an estimated date of 2034 as the beginning of the end. That would likely bother most people, given that we are not that far away from that date.

Aside from being around the corner, why else was 2034 such an important date?

This article predicted a tipping point in consumer debt, various economic bubbles, and other financial hurdles, leading to a snowball effect that would make 2008 look like a walk in the park.

Because I am an optimist, I generally do not put a lot of merit into doomsday scenarios, as we always tend to "figure it out"; however, this one was based in math rather than emotional assertion. Anything based in math has my full attention and consideration. While I lay in bed, my mind swirled around the idea as I fell asleep.

The following morning was Sunday. I woke up and began preparing for church. As I did so, I had a nagging sense, like a headline in my brain that said, "you know how to fix it." As I sat it church, attended Sunday School, and various other Sunday routines, this thought became stronger. "You know how to fix it!"

As I continued the day, going to my parent's house to eat dinner as we do every Sunday, the feeling did not subside until late in the evening when I finally realized something. My research could fix the impending financial Armageddon faced by a financial society built on promoting linear growth with compounding debt.

At around 8pm on February 24th, 2019, eight words came to mind clear as day: "Look to Compound Interest, it will fix it." Where was this voice coming from? As I got the kids ready for bed, "Look to Compound Interest" was on the forefront of my mind. I put them to bed, kissed my wife, and told her I needed to work on something. As everyone went to bed, I got my laptop out with pen and paper and began.

Compound Interest! That's the key. From around 8:30 p.m. to 1:00 a.m., I focused on the data of the current US household debt, income, cost of living, inflation, and various other factors that play a role in the lives of the American population.

As I reviewed the data, I saw the flaw; why it was unsustainable and on the verge of collapse. Our money was never truly compounding. It was a linear system. No matter how good the investment was, or how much debt we paid off, or how many rentals we managed, it would inevitably underperform because it wasn't based on the Science of Compound Interest. Although this flaw was huge, I could clearly see how to fix it. Always Be Compounding!

After researching the issue and embracing the hypothesis that compounding would "fix" this financial implosion, it was time to stress-test it. Would it prove out?

With all the financial data available to me, I plugged hundreds of scenarios into $y = a(1 + r)^x$, maximized through the MPI™ algorithm of Secure Leverage, and guess what happened? It fixed it! No matter the debt load or income levels of an individual, Paying Yourself First and compounding fixed every situation. It wasn't immediate, but with enough time, it provided prosperity to anyone. The rate of growth became more rapid over time, eventually producing enough wealth for all. The answer was so simple, Always Be Compounding!

Although for the prior 16 months I had been educating people on how the power of Compound Interest could benefit their individual lives, on the early morning of February 25th, 2019, it became my calling. It is what I am supposed to do: finish Einstein's work by educating the world that Compound Interest is truly the 8th Wonder of the World, the most powerful force in the Universe, and can fix any situation, no matter how severe.

In that moment, sitting on the couch in my living room at around 2:00 a.m., my mind was open, I saw how this would play out, the possibility and probability of a compounding-focused society that would become the vehicle to provide happiness and freedom unlike the world has ever experienced before.

My name is Curtis Ray. I'm a money scientist and conservative risk-taker. I believe the power of Compound Interest is truly the most powerful force in the universe. My calling is to teach the world how Compound Interest is fully achieved. I have a clear vision and understanding about what needs to happen so that financial security is not only accomplished by you as an individual but expanded throughout our country to every family including children and future generations to come.

I know Compound Interest will enable us to climb our way out of this debt-hole we have dug for ourselves, and it will also be the means to many other great advancements in society.

In my lifetime, we will see our veterans taken care of, our elderly living in comfort, our less fortunate having opportunities never seen before, and the compounding effects of progress and money will spread across the world. Compound Interest is the means through which every person has access to success and freedom, it is not a redistribution scheme, but a path to abundance for those who but take the time to understand it. It is the universal success formula available to all.

These three words can fix almost anything: Always Be Compounding!

Everyone Ends Up Rich! It really is that straightforward and predictable.

How do I know this is all going to happen? Because I can already see it!

"The Best Way to Predict the Future is to Create It!"

Abraham Lincoln

NOTES/THOUGHTS

Additional Testimonials

"Learning about MPI™ and Compound Interest has been one of the most valuable things I've learned in my life. I have a master's degree in engineering, yet I had never seen anything like this before. I'm extremely grateful and thankful to have met Curtis Ray, the creator of MPI™. Albert Einstein wasn't lying when he called Compound Interest the most powerful force in the Universe and the 8th Wonder of the World. Taking the time to understand MPI™ is without a doubt the best thing you can do for yourself and your family."
—*Angie Merget, Scottsdale, Arizona*

"I've known Curtis and his family for a long time. Their work ethic is intense. I've competed in sports with Curtis. While very competitive, he's fair and a good sportsman. I've seen his mind churn to develop MPI™ for the maximum benefit to the client. After evaluating MPI™ for myself and my clients, I've determined it to be a game changing innovation that can help save the next generation of retirees from failed retirement plans."
— *Spencer Alldredge, CFP®, Mesa, Arizona*

"My husband and I were searching for a way to make Compound Interest work to our advantage. When we saw Curtis Ray present the MPI™ system we knew instantly this was THE BEST route for us. We have complete faith in Curtis Ray and MPI™. We are more than happy with our experience and results."
— *Ronda Parker, State Highway, Texas*

"Because MPI™ takes away all the stress and anxiety typically associated with financial planning, I am incredibly grateful to have found Curtis Ray. Not only are we as a family setup for our best possible financial future, Curtis has transformed the way I advise my clients. There is, quite simply, *nothing else that checks all the boxes and adheres to all of the 5 Rules of Wealth. By simply following the math, I have full confidence knowing that I'm doing what's best for my clients and my family."*

— **Steve Thurmond, CFF®, Chattanooga, TN**

With help from Curtis Ray, I have discovered the rules that govern wealth and the brilliant strategy at the foundation of Maximum Premium Indexing or MPI™. In the past, I simply set aside a portion of my income hoping that someday I'd retire with a substantial nest egg, neglecting to understand the details of my own plan and the inherent fallacies underlying the traditional financial planning industry.

I first approached Curtis after one of his motivating speeches about wealth management and told him, "I need your help!" He smiled and handed me a signed copy of his book, "Everyone Ends Up Poor!" Total game changer! The principles of paying yourself first; securing your investment; Compound Interest; and, Secure Leverage, have withstood the test of time and are positioned perfectly within MPI™ to maximize retirement income, regardless of one's financial situation.

This revolutionary financial strategy provides peace of mind and the opportunity for anyone to achieve financial freedom in a world full of get-rich-quick financial investment schemes. Slow, steady, AND secure always wins the race!

— **Jake Troutman, Gilbert, Arizona**

"1 million dollars is not enough for retirement." These were the words my wife and I heard from a financial planner that crushed us! What is the point of retirement planning if we can never retire?! We were introduced to Curtis' first book and our eyes were opened! The problem wasn't the amount we were contributing but where we were putting our money. We will now have a better income, earlier retirement, and greater freedom through MPI™. Never have we felt more exited and secure for our future. We want everyone to feel the way we will.

— **Jeff Blosil, West Richland, Washington**

"I have worked closely with financial planners for years. The MPI™ system takes traditional, and often times overly complex retirement planning, and

simplifies it for the masses. Now, it isn't just the wealthy that have access to a bright financial future. This conservative yet extremely efficient approach allows for investors to feel confident that they have minimized risk while maximizing long-term growth."

— **Porter Shumway, Mesa, Arizona**

"I've always been pretty conservative in my investments, mostly sticking to real estate and an IRA. Curtis and MPI™ have completely changed the way I think about money and investing. MPI™ makes my conservative mind feel at ease but gives me hope in actually having the retirement I dream of!"

— **Jared Maybon, Boise, Idaho**

"I read the book Everyone Ends Up Poor! *in a single sitting. The concepts resonated with me and made immediate sense. I emailed Curtis and was texted back within minutes, which was followed up with a cell phone conversation. After completing some of my own research and calculations, I was confident of my retirement and long-term financial future planning. I had a structured and realistic outline of how I would obtain financial independence. The Equation was easily understood and applied, the key and most exciting part was the Compound Interest and the technique the MPI™ program incorporated to grow wealth. Everything clicked, all my questions were answered, and I started my adventure with MPI™. It is as advertised, and I could not be more pleased."*

— **Steve Larson, Chandler Arizona.**

"The beauty of MPI™ is in its simplicity. Never has there been such a simple, secure way to compound and leverage your money to create true exponential growth. Curtis has created a system that will allow anyone to become wealthy if you just follow the rules of wealth/money. I am honored and privileged to be partnered with SunCor Financial and Curtis Ray in the mission to "rescue retirement" so my clients can have a Life In Retirement©."

— **Leon King, Greenville, South Carolina**

"I was just like you, intrigued by what I had heard. Financially, I knew I wasn't on the path I was hoping for (even though I was in the finance industry) and I didn't feel like I had a clear way forward. There's just so much insecurity and risk in mainstream financial strategies! Curtis's first book, Everyone Ends Up Poor!, was my first step. It helped clarify the current state of the "industry" and gave me hope a better future was possible. After my own extensive research, I came to understand MPI™ as the evolution of money, building more tax-free spendable income for my future while also possessing the security of the 0% floor. Knowledge is powerful as we apply it in our lives. Take these teachings, follow the simple rules of wealth in your life, and exponential growth is the outcome!

—*Rob Duve, Mesa, Arizona*

Afterword

Thank you for reading *The Lost Science of Compound Interest!*

"An Investment in Knowledge Pays the Best Interest."
Ben Franklin

I once read a definition of success that went something like "success is doing our best; and when we know better, we then do better."

Now that you know the steps to take to secure your future and that of your family, what will you do? Will you start today? Will you Pay Yourself First? Will you ensure your money is secure? Will you securely leverage?

After that, will you share the investment of knowledge so someone else can also enjoy the freedom you've found?

Right now, you probably thought of someone that has struggled—perhaps sincerely believing that life will never give them abundance no matter how hard they work: Give this book to them. Let them have your copy.

Then, as you think of the people in your family, in your circle, and others that look to you for guidance, get them a copy. If you believe, as I do, that being a great friend or family member is about helping others become financially independent, share your knowledge, experience, and belief in the power of Compound Interest. It could change their life forever!

#AlwaysBeCompounding

Thank you!

Curtis Ray

Curtis@CurtisRay.com

Your Customized Financial Plan

SunCor Financial, LLC, founded in 2014, is based in Gilbert, Arizona. Curtis Ray, owner, founder, and CEO, has a passion for educating all regarding the phenomenon of Compound Interest, the Five Rules of Wealth, and the revolutionary system of MPI™.

SunCor Financial serves families and individuals across the country to design and implement a long-term secure financial plan. SunCor Financial has six core financial plans that provide value and a path to compounding for all those who want to receive its benefits.

Through education and understanding of the elements of Compound Interest, everyone can achieve the financial freedom they desire. No matter if you're just starting or if you've been saving for many years in the traditional system, we have a solution for you. We've developed a framework of models to meet you where you are right now in order to help you on the road to becoming a Pure Compounder. The six systems are:

- MPI™ Traditional (regular contributions to retire in 15–30 years)

- MPI™ Accelerated (large contribution to retire in 3–15 years)

- MPI™ Children (small contributions for college savings and financial security through life)

- MPI™ Legacy (large contributions for retirement income, tax-free wealth transfer and legacy planning)

- MPI™ Whole Life Upgrade (upgrading the outdated Infinite Banking Concept/ Bank On Yourself system)

- MPI™ Business Protection (long-term security for business viability and liquidity)

For more information or help designing your plan,
please contact us at:

SunCor
FINANCIAL

459 N. Gilbert Rd #A-145
Gilbert, AZ 85234
(480) 530–5840

Info@SunCorFinancial.com
www.SunCorFinancial.com
www.CompoundInterest.com

Made in United States
Orlando, FL
18 August 2024